¡ The Jesus Letters!

¡The Jesus Letters!
Letters from an Innocent Abroad in Ireland

Eanna Brophy

BLACKWATER PRESS

Editor
Ríona MacNamara

Design & Layout
Paula Byrne

ISBN
0 86121 718 7

© – Eanna Brophy 1995

Produced in Ireland by
Blackwater Press,
c/o Folens Publishers,
8 Broomhill Business Park,
Tallaght, Dublin 24.

To Yvonne

Chapter 1

November 1994

Ola mama y papa!

Juel! Jere I am in Irlanda at last! But I do not theenk I wish to stay jere, mama y papa, because it is a very strange country. I theenk everybody jere is mad, mama y papa!

Jwhen I arrive at the aeroporto in Dublino there is nobody to meet me. Jwhere ees my Irish family, I ask myself? Then I ask the security man at the door eef he see any bodies looking for a Spanish au pair. He look me up and down and tell me I am pulling his leg. This I think is a strange thing to say, because I am standing on the other side of the counter with two suitcases and a rucksack.

Then he say something even stranger. He call his friend over and tell him that Julio Iglesias jere is lost. I look around very surprised, but do not see Julio anyjwhere. I am very disappointed because I want to ask him about something I read about him and ten thousand women in a magazine. (It is not important, mama y papa, and anyjway I do not believe him, Julio I mean.)

The other man ask me jwhat is the name of my Irish family and I tell him it is the McClancys. Then he go to a telephone and say he will find out if they are looking for me. Then he ask me my name. I tell him I am Jésus.

Haysoos? he say.

Jaysoos! say his friend. Then they both bless themselves and laugh.

Anyjway, mama y papa, the loudspeakers in the airport ask many times if there is any bodies called McClancy there to meet Haysoos from Spain but nobody comes. Then the men tell me where the taxis are and I show the driver the address of my Irish family.

Jaysoos! he say, rubbing his hands and taking my cases, but how did he know my name? Everybody in Dublino seems to know my name, mama y papa, it is very strange.

The driver open the door for me and say, we are not dealing with muck here.

I tell him no, the taxi is very clean except for the old World Cup pictures. He laugh and drive out onto the main road.

I practise some more English on him. Eet ees very nice day today, I say to the driver.

Yes, he say, but you're lucky you were not jere the other week, the whole road was blocked by a shower.

I say I do not understand how a shower could block a whole road.

He say he mean this shower was from the team.

Sometimes, mama y papa, I do not think they speak the best English in the world jere like Father Ignacio tell you.

I think sometimes it is not English at all.

Then the driver tell me he know Spain well. He ask me do I know Paddy's Bar in Fuengalora. I tell him I do not know that place. Then he ask me if I know the Shamrock Bar in Benidorm, and when I tell him I am never in Benidorm he look at me in the mirror and ask if I am sure I am Spanish.

I tell him I am from Madrid, and he say he thought I was from Barcelona. Then he laugh to himself and say don't mention the war.

I have not said anything about the war, but some parts of Dublin look like they have been bombed many times. We go past some very big apartments, just like in Spain. There are many of them, and they all look the same. Soon I think I am passing the same ones again and again, and my head is spinning.

There is a newspaper in the front seat and I try to read the words. SPRING TO PULL PLUG ON ALBERT, it say.

What is this spring, I ask the driver.

He is Mr Clean, he say, and Albert tried to pull a fast one on him but now the shoe is on the other foot.

I tell him I do not understand what he is saying, and he say welcome to the club.

I look out and see no club, but there are some broken-down buildings and steps down to a basement. I ask him is that the club. He laughs and say you can say that again. But before I do he says there are certainly a lot of private members there. The police have them all on video, he say. Then he laugh so much I think he is going to crash the taxi, mama y papa! I tell him to be careful or he will be knocking the shop, but this makes him laugh again.

Later we are passing by a big plaza with a palazzo in the middle. He tell me this is the Government. I say I must visit it some day while I am jere, and he say it is run by Q Tours.

Anyway, mama y papa, I am mixed up even more when we arrive at the big house jere near the mountains. The house of the McClancy family is trying to be like a Spanish hacienda. It has big concrete balconies every-where – even on the roof of the garage – and there is a big archway at the front door.

I ring the bell, and tell the driver to wait, and he say he is not going anywhere, pal.

I ring the bell again and then I knock on the big knocker.

At last the door is opened by a fat man who is trousering. Excuse me, mama y papa, that should be panting because he have been running to the door.

Jhello, I say to him, I am your au pair Jésus!

Suffering Haysoos! he say.

I tell him I am quite well, thank you.

No, he say, I mean if you're an au pair then I'm Gerry Adams.

3

I tell him that Father Ignacio said this was the address of the McClancy family jwhere I am to stay.

But there must be some mistake, he say. You've got the right house, but it's Sunday and you're not a girl!

Just then a woman in a very nice suit with nice black hair is coming out into the hallway also. She is carrying a small case. She smile and say, heaven is above and who is this?

Jhello, Mrs McClancy, I say, I very glad to meet you.

She laugh and say she is certainly not Mrs McClancy. Then she frown and say to Mr McClancy, I thought you said we would not be disturbed?

The taxi-driver then say to Mr McClancy that the fare will be forty lids, boss.

Then they say a lot of things to each other very rapidly so that I do not understand it all. But Mr McClancy is saying to him something about cowboys.

The driver say, that's some squaw you have there, sunshine.

Mr McClancy then pay the fare.

I go in and wait. The woman who is not Mrs McClancy drive off in a sporting car. She is a fast woman, because she nearly pass out the taxi in the driveway.

Then Mr McClancy make phone call. Jhello, dear, he say, guess who's jere? Haysoos! He then say no, he is not swearing, but the au pair is a he not a she.

Chapter 2

Ola Mama y papa!

Jwell, jere I am in my room at the home of the McClancys. It is not so bad, but smaller than my room in Madrid and much smaller than my room in El Finca de Naranjuez. I bang my head off the roof a lot because it slant down suddenly. It is the room of their eldest daughter. But don't worry, mama y papa, she is not jere. She is gone to America and will not be back for a long time, Mrs McClancy say jwhen she show me the room. Mr McClancy say maybe she not come jhome at all unless she get a visa from Mr Morrison, but his jwife say not to talk like that because she was talking to Jean about it in the park. Mr McClancy roll his eyes. He do that a lot, mama y papa.

They have two other children, but I do not meet them yet. They are visiting their uncle in the country. I ask if she live on a big estate, and they look funny at each other. Then Mr McClancy say, yes, you could say that. I tell him my grandmama live on a grand estate and they look funny at each other again.

But first I tell you about jwhat happen when the real Mrs McClancy come jhome last night. She drive up in a big car and skid on the gravel at the door. She nearly hit the pillars and the car of Mr McClancy. Then she jump out of the car and run in and start sniffing the air in the jhallway.

Jwhat kind of au pair jhave they sent us? she ask her husband. She say, I thought you said it's not a girl.

He nod his head. Then jwho is wearing the perfume, she ask?

Mr McClancy shrug his head and look at me. I open my mouth to say something but he speak first.

Spanish after-shave, say Mr McClancy.

His jwife sniff again then look at me. Jwell, she say at last, at least we won't have the trouble we jhad with the Swedish one.

Then she say I suppose you are jhungry and I say *si*. She say that she was afraid of that. They show me where the kitchen is and Mrs McClancy gives me bread and some jham and tomatoes. I ask if it is the cook's night off but they both laugh.

The bread jhere is very strange, mama y papa. They call it pan just like jhome, but it is very thin slices. Mrs McClancy say it is Margaret's bread, but it is named after another saint. I eat twelve slices before she take it away suddenly.

Everybody jhere watches television all the time, mama y papa! It is a show called *The Shenanigans* I think. That's what Mr McClancy call it whenever he switch it on. Everybody in the show sit around in a big room and shout at everybody else. There is a man with a bing-bong in the middle, but nobody knows jwhat he is there for. I ask Mr and Mrs McClancy jwhat are the rules of the game but they say shh, shh!

Jhere is jwhat I think is jhappening. There is a man called Alberto and he jhas to find the right piece of paper before he is eliminated by the man with the bing-bongs. Alberto has many pieces of paper in front of jhim. He is many times picking them up and reading bits from them, and then putting them down again. Everybody else is shouting at him. He looks down for another piece of paper.

The man sitting beside him, his name is nearly the same. It is El Bert, I think, but he does not look very jhappy at all.

There are many women in this television game, too. They are all called Mary. Except the ones who are called Liz.

But everybody is watching El Dic. He is like a matador, putting in the sword after many gestures with the cloak and the dagger. Grandmama would love to watch this game, because it would remind her of the old days.

But, mama y papa, what a shock I got next! I am watching the game and laughing at it, and I ask them if all the television games are as good as this one. Then Mr McClancy say this is not a game, this is the Shaggin Government. (I try to find this phrase later in book but it is not there.)

Then they explain to me that it's all about a Thorny General. I tell them we used to jhave problems with them in Spain, but now we have a king instead. Mr McClancy say Ireland jhave a president instead, who is much more powerful. She think she is God Almighty, he say. But Mrs McClancy say he is just jealous because she is better than any man.

Chapter 3

Mama y papa!

Now I think I really want to come jhome.

I jhave at last met the children of the McClancys.

I wake up this morning and there is a horrible noise outside my door. At first I think I am dreaming I am on grandmama's ranch because the noise is like jwhen they are killing the pigs. But no, mama y papa, at last I get out of bed and bump my jhead off the ceiling. I fall asleep then for a few minutes, but when my eyes open the noise is still there outside.

Then I open the door and look out. There are two bodies rolling around on the top of the stairs. Maybe they are buglers I think at first, because I jhear Mrs McClancy say last night that many jhouses jhere have been bugled. But then Mr McClancy come out of his bedroom shouting jwhat in the name of Haysoos is going on, and the two bodies stop fighting.

Then I see it is a boy and a girl, I think. Because, mama y papa, the boy look like a girl and the girl look like a boy. They look at me and I look at them and they look back at me.

Then one of them say, who are you? Mr McClancy say Haysoos.

The boy and the girl say he should not be saying that word. Then I say that is my name.

Then the boy and the girl start laughing and laughing and I am afraid they are falling down the stairs. They shout Haysoos, Haysoos at each other and jump up and down.

Then Mrs McClancy come out of her room. I get a fright because I do not know who she is. She look all funny without the paint on her face. She look like the English queen Elizabeth, mama y papa. Not the second one but the first one who fight with our king. But the Irish people must be like the English king and queen, mama y papa, because the mother and the father jhave their own bedroom each one.

Mrs McClancy say, I see you jhave met the twins. I look at them again but they do not look like twins.

Mama y papa, they do not look like being humans!

Their names are Theo and Cleo and they are eleven years old. But I think they are not like Spanish children who are eleven, because the boy have long jhair and earrings and wear boots with the jhigh jheels. And jhis sister has short jhair like a crew cut and she wear rough clothes and big boots. She look like the man who kill the pigs for grandmama.

They stop laughing after a while. Then I say jhello and they start laughing again. Mr McClancy say shut up and he look at jhis watch and go downstairs.

The girl ask me why I am not a girl, and the boy say don't be silly, there is no girls called Haysoos.

Then Mrs McClancy say not to mind them. I say that I think that it is my au pair job to mind them, but she say no, I don't mean don't mind them, I mean don't mind them.

She say that Mr McClancy and Mrs McClancy (which is her) are very busy people. He goes to work in his office and she jhas a boutique, so it will be my job to mind the jhouse and clean the dishes and make the beds and get the lunch ready for the twins jwhen they come jhome from school.

I am going to say but jwhat about my English classes jwhen the phone rings downstairs and Mr McClancy answer it. Mrs McClancy run into her bedroom and pick up another phone. Then she say in a loud voice, how would I know? This is not the met service.

Mr McClancy shout up the stairs get off the line, it's important business call, but his wife shout back, then why did that woman ask is the coast clear?

Mr McClancy is now saying into phone, jhello, jhello no you jhave a wrong number madam. Then he hang up and say it was a wrong number. Mrs McClancy throw a shoe at him, but it miss and jhit the front door window.

She shout at jhim that he is at it again. He shout back that it is his business, and she say if he minded his real business he would not be in trouble. He ask jwhat trouble and she say never mind, she jhear things.

Then he say oh yes you jhear all sorts of things from your friend Lady Bountyful.

She say don't call her that, and he say, you and your so-called charities.

Then she is saying we do good work, and he is saying charity begins at jhome. She say jhow would you know, you are never jhere.

That is jwhen we smell the smoke. It is coming from Cleo's room, where she jhas lit the fire. (They do not jhave a fireplace in the room, mama y papa.)

Then everybody start screaming and running around and throwing water. Soon the fire is out, but I am very, very wet.

Atishoo, mama y papa, I think I am getting the chimney, which is another word for the flue.

You see, I am learning!

Chapter 4

Ola!

Jwell, mama y papa, maybe I stay jhere in Irlanda after all. Today I went to my English class for the first time and there are many other students jhere from our country and from other countries.

But I do not understand the transport system very well yet. I wait for a bus to the school. I am the only one at the bus stop but the bus not stop. Instead, it go past very fast, but the driver wave two fingers at me. I think this means there is another bus coming in two minutes, but it does not come for jhalf an jhour. This driver stops and lets me on, but he say Haysoos, I thought youse lot were gone home since the summer.

Our teacher's name is Conchubhair and he has long hair and a horse's tail. He has travelled all over the world and he tells us many stories about strange places called Nepal and Nirvana.

I ask him why he travel so much and he said the grass is always greener far away. Then he laugh a funny little laugh to himself and roll his eyes. I tell him that we always learn the grass in Ireland is greener than any other place in the whole world, but he just laugh again and do the same thing with his eyes.

Jwhen he does this, Mercedes laughs so much she nearly is falling off her chair.

But, mama y papa, I forget I did not tell you yet about Mercedes. She is from the Basque country but very nice. She have brown eyes and brown curly hair and she laugh a lot. Jwhen I tell her about Mr and Mrs McClancy I think she is going to fall off her chair again, but I catch her arm just in time.

She is living in another part of Dublin. It is called the Norside. Our teacher Conchubhair say he has never been there. He say he has been fighting with crocodiles in Australia and was once bitten by a dalai lama in Peru, but wild horses would not drag jhim to the Norside.

We ask jhim jwhy, and he say because there are too many wild horses there already.

But Mercedes tells him that she is staying with a very nice family. They have many friends who visit the jhouse at all times of the day and night. She thinks they go to many parties, and some of them are fancy-dress, because one night she look out and see them all putting on funny rubber masks – Ronald Reagan and Mickey Mouse etc. – and driving off in a big jeep like the one grandmama drive on her rancho.

Conchubhair ask Mercedes jwhat does the father of the family work at, and she say that is what she does not understand. She thinks they have a laundry, because she hears them saying that the money has come from the laundry but she never sees a van with the name. She thinks they also bury dead people. Undertakers they are called here. That's a new word I learned today. Mercedes tells the class that undertakers drive around in a big heist. Conchubhair say no, no, the word is hearse. But Mercedes say that is not the way her family say it. Maybe they have a different accent on the Norside?

Anyway, mama y papa, jwhen I tell Mrs McClancy about Mercedes and jwhere she is staying, she look funny and say, the poor girl.

I say she is not poor, her father own many shops in San Sebastian, but Mrs McClancy say that is not jwhat she mean jwhen she say the poor girl.

Then Theo and Cleo run in and start fighting, so I am not able to find out jwhat is the difference between jwhat they mean and jwhat they say.

But that is the trouble with Irlanda, mama y papa! I watch the television again last night, and cannot understand anything. They are all talking again about the Thorny General. I tell you about him already. But now there are two Thorny Generals, mama y papa!

Even in Madrid, we never had more than one at a time.

But Mr McClancy explain that one Thorny General is going to be the President. No, not of the country, he say. Robbo would never stand for that. Mrs McClancy say don't call jher that, she is going to come and open the new heritage and craft centre later this year. Mr McClancy nearly spill his drink. Jwhat heritage centre is that, he ask. She say the one in the old school the nuns are selling. Her committee is going to get the school, she says, for the benefit of the community and to create job opportunities.

Mr McClancy put down his drink very loudly and I think the little table is going to crack. He start to talk in a very loud voice. Jwhat would you know about job opportunities, he ask. Then he answer himself by saying sweet and other words I do not like to write down, mama y papa.

Mrs McClancy say that not true, she run a boutique, and he snort and say pin money. I do not know what pin money is, I must ask Conchubhair at the next class.

Then he say the only real jobs in this country came from building. Getting a shovel in your hand and jwheelbarrow in the other and a few bricks in the other is the only way to the top of the ladder, he say very loudly.

Mrs McClancy say yes, he could do that because he was always a contortionist, but that he was never in a wet trench with cement up to jhis ears like jher father jwhen he started. Then suddenly Mr McClancy start to sing very loudly a song about some soldiers called McAlpine's fusileers.

Mrs McClancy tell him to stop, stop, and he say it's a pity he did not leave jher some more of his money jwhen he go, but she say it is just as well or he would jhave given it all to his friends the accountants. I think bookmaker is another word for accountant jhere, mama y papa.

Anyway, the nuns jhere in Irlanda must be very rich, mama y papa, because Mr McClancy say they are sitting on a goldmine. He also say he bets they will forget about heritage and go for hard cash. He says that he and the Mother Superior speak the same language. Then he pick up the paper quickly and read it.

I wonder jwhat language that is, mama y papa, because I do not think it is English like I learn back at school.

Chapter 5

Ola!

Today there is much excitement in the McClancy jhome and all over Irlanda! Albert jhave lost the game of Shenanigans I told you about earlier. He could not find the right piece of paper, and all his friends are very sad. They blame each other for not giving him the paper, especially the woman they call Maria de la Gegonquin. She nearly cry on the television, especially because she have hoped to be the next leader, but she have being beaten by El Bert. Now he will be the Taoiseach, which is an Irish word like Caudillo. Did you know they jhave another language jhere as well as English? Not many people speak it. (Mercedes say not many people speak English either but she is always joking.)

Anyway, mama y papa, jwhen it say on the television that El Bert is to be the next Caudillo, I mean El Taoiseach, Mr McClancy say a funny word. It is *wayaboyah*. I take out my notebook and ask him to say it again. He laugh and say wayaboyah! And he punch the air. I ask him jwhat does wayaboyah mean, and he say it means good man yourself.

Mrs McClancy come in then and say what's that about good man, I hope he's not involved in any of this.

Mr McClancy say no it was just an expression, and Mrs McClancy say thank God because he cost us enough already. Then she look at El Bert on the screen and say, what he looking so smug about? He look like the cat that got the cream. I write that down in my notebook. Then she say something else about him and Mr McClancy tell me not to write it down.

Then Mrs McClancy ask where are Theo and Cleo. I say they go to bed early because they are very tired. She thinks that is strange. Usually, she say, they stay up and want to watch Beavis and Butthead on the television. She say I am doing a good job if they are so tired they want to go to bed early. Mr McClancy say maybe I've been giving them some of her little blue pills and then he laugh. Then I say no the red ones and he stop laughing. Which red ones, Mrs McClancy shout, but I tell them I am just joking. I do not see any red pills really. But they do not think it is funny.

Just then the front door bell ring. I open it and get a big surprise. There is a big policeman and also Theo and Cleo.

Do these really live jhere, he asks me. I say yes and call Mrs McClancy. She scream jwhen she see them, especially the blood on Theo's face. The policeman explain that he did not believe them jwhen they said they lived in this big jhouse. It not the kind of place you usually find joyriders, he say. I take out my notebook again and ask Mrs McClancy what it is this word joyriders. She say shut up.

Then she smile and say won't you come in, guard. Then Mr McClancy come to door and start to shout. Are you accusing my children of stealing cars, he say very loud. Just exactly jwhat car did they steal, he ask. The guard take out jhis notebook and say the car and the number.

Then Mr McClancy scream. That is my car, he say, and he try to hit Theo but he run behind Cleo and she get hit instead. She start to cry and tell the policeman to save her. Mrs McClancy say shut up again and shuts the door behind the policeman.

Then they tell him it was a mistake, that Theo and Cleo did not mean to take the car out of the garden. The policeman say that all very well, but they were doing ninety down the Shankill bypass.

Mr McClancy then look as though he is having a heart attack. He shout at me I thought you were supposed to be an ofecking pair. But I tell jhim the twins were asleep so I went to study my English words.

He say he will give me some English words I never heard before but the policeman say now now. He tell them jhe will not put the twins in jail this time, but he hopes they learned a lesson. Mr McClancy say you can say that again, but the policeman does not.

Jwhen he is gone, I ask Mr McClancy to tell me the new English words, but I do not understand what he says.

Mrs McClancy is looking out through the curtains and saying why do they have to use the blue lights and the siren? Then she look around for Theo and Cleo, but they have locked themselves in their bedrooms.

Chapter 6

Ola, mam y dad!

Jwell, I had fun at my English class today! Jwhen our teacher, Conchubhair, ask if anyone learn any new words yesterday I say yes, joyriding. He ask how I learned that, and I tell the whole class all about the twins and the car and the policeman. Conchubhair ask me if I am sure I really live on the Southside.

I say yes because I have jheard Mrs McClancy and her friends tell laughing and joking about the Northside (that is really the Norside I told you about in my other letter). One of her friends say how do you know a Northsider in a Merc? And then she answer – because it is a taxi. Then all her friends laugh.

Nobody in the class laugh jwhen I tell them. Conchubhair says that it is because she tell it wrong. He say it should be jwhat do you say to a Northsider in a Merc and the answer is – the airport. But nobody in the class laugh again.

The teacher shrug and say never mind, we will pick up the nuances later. I tell jhim that is what Mrs McClancy call the twins – she says she has to pick up the nuances from school. I hear her say this at the meeting she has with her friends in the jhouse. She calls it the Committee, but Mr McClancy call it some other word that sounds like cousin or oven. Coven. I must ask my teacher what that word means.

Anyway, the Committee are all ladies and one man. They are having a meeting to get ready for Christmas, I think, because jwhen I come in from the kitchen with tea

and biscuits for them, I jhear them asking Mrs McClancy jwhere did she get the toy boy. Just then I come in and Mrs McClancy look funny and say shh, shh, and the other ladies all laugh.

I nearly laugh too, because they are funny-looking ladies. I think at first they are not Irish ladies at all, because they all jhave the skin of the peasants. Some of them look like leather – you know the old saddles on the burros on my grandmother's rancho.

The man with them have white skin. Jwhen I put down the tray, he tells me I am a very handsome young caballero. Mrs McClancy start coughing and nearly spill her tea. She say, Give over, Cedric.

I do not think they have a royal family in Ireland, but now I am not so sure, mama y papa, because later I hear Mr McClancy ask Mrs McClancy was that old queen at the meeting again.

Another thing they talk about at the meeting was joyriding. One lady ask Mrs McClancy did someone try to steal one of their cars because she sees the Garda calling at the door (that is jwhat they call the policemen jhere, though I hear Mrs McClancy use another word last night). Mrs McClancy laugh and say no, no, it was a false alarm.

But then I say no the alarm did not go off at all because Theo and Cleo had the keys to the car. The man, Cedric say jwhat do you mean, and I say they were caught doing ninety on the bypass. Just then Mrs McClancy say gosh is that the time? I jhave to hurry and pick up those nuances from school.

Conchubhair laugh jwhen I tell him this and says the word is nuisances.

It is a different word all together, he says. Many words jhere are different all together, mama y papa. Earlier at the meeting of Mrs McClancy's committee, she tell them they will have to get off their burros and move fast to stop the nuns' gallop because they are very fond of writing quickly. I do not know jwhat this mean either, but she say you know jhow they like to make a fast book.

Her friends ask is someone else after the building too, and Mrs McClancy say she hear rumours that someone want to build jhouses and shops there.

They ask who but she say she not sure. Then they talk about some word called zoning. They say it is not zoned for shops and jhouses. But someone says that can always be changed.

Then Cedric say well thank heaven at least it is not zoned for a halting site, and they all laugh.

Later I ask Conchubhair what is zoning and rezoning and he say it is something you do if you have the right people in your pocket. I ask jhim what does that mean and he tell me the class is too short to explain the nuisances.

Chapter 7

December

Ola mama y papa!

Today we learn about politics. In the class, Conchubhair (whose name is spelt very funny, but pronounced even more funny) ask us jwhat do we know about Irish politicians. Mercedes put up jher hand at once, and say they are all a shower of gobshites.

Concubhair say that is a very interesting idiom, and she say her Irish family say that all the time when they are watching the television and she ask them what is the difference between the parties. Then she ask jwhat does the idiom mean and he say that's for the advanced classes. But he tell us all not to use it, because some people might not like to be called that. I ask jhim what is wrong with the word shower and he say that not the word he's talking about. Then he laugh and say don't call anyone a politician either.

Then he go to the blackboard and explain to us jwhat are the different political parties in Ireland. It is not at all like Spain, mama y papa.

First there is the biggest party. It is called Fianna Fáil and it was founded, he tell us, by a Spanish man. His name was DeValera, and they all called jhim the long fellow or Dev for short.

I ask jhow this Spanish man come to Ireland and he say he is not sure, maybe God sent him. Dev, he say was very fond of the dancing, and he founded this party because he want everyone in Ireland to go out in the

21

roads and dance. Mercedes ask was it not dangerous with all the traffic, and Conchubhair say nobody could afford a car jwhen Dev was there, so it was safe to dance on the roads.

But now, he say, everyone want their own Mercedes.

Everyone laugh when he make this joke, except Mercedes, who go red.

The teacher say this party is still having a dancing tradition, because the last leader, Alberto, was also fond of dancing and he built big barns all over the country for the people to come in off the roads. Sometimes there were five thousand people in the barns, he say, but you would think there were only two.

He tell us there was another leader called El Seejay, who was not being so good at the dancing, because it was the taps that tripped jhim up in the end. The new leader is El Bert, but nobody know yet whether El Dic will dance with him.

The next big party is called Fine Gael, and the leader do donkey noises jwhen he laugh. Right now he is laughing a lot on the television because he may be the new leader of the whole country. I ask Conchubhair if they are good at dancing, but I don't think so because he say they certainly fell on their feet.

Then there is the Labour party, who are led by El Dic and his friend Ho Chi Quinn. Conchubhair say they are very quick to move from one side of the floor to the other.

There are some small parties, too. There is one called Progressive Democrats. Conchubhair say this is a new party. He is not sure about their dancing, but they wag their fingers a lot.

And there is another party called Democratic Left. It is led by Princess de Rosa – but, mama y papa, it is a man with a beard.

When they jhave an election jhere, they do not just give one vote to one man or woman. Everybody jhas lots of votes to give, so the elections can take a very long time.

Maybe that is why they are not having one now. Conchubhair say the system is called PR which stands for two big words I do not understand. When I tell him this he say don't worry, nobody else in Irlanda does either.

Chapter 8

Oh my jhead, mama y papa! Last night we went to an Irish pub.

You know the Irish pub we see every year in the Eurovision Song Contest? The one jwhere everyone is playing violins and concertinas and funny pipes and singing and eating oysters? And the sun is shining outside on the blue sea jwhere men in caps are rowing black boats full of lobsters?

The pub we go to is not being like that. And it is not like the BageLuz in Madrid where I meet my friends. First of all, it is night-time and second it is raining. And jwhen someone start to sing the barman shout no singing, we're watching the football. It is the World Cup when Ireland beat Italy.

I ask him for some oysters and he look at me very slowly and then ask me do I think he look like Patrick Bleedin Gilbow. I tell him I do not as I have never met this Patrick. I tell him I am from Madrid and he say that explain it. He say the Spanish people have eaten all their own oysters and now they are coming to Ireland looking for more, the way they have hoovered all the fish out of the sea.

I tell him I use a hoover in Mrs McClancy's house, but never try using it for fishing. Another man at the bar ask me jwhere did I park my Armada, but I tell him I do not drive.

But why are we in this pub, mama y papa? Jwell, Conchubhair our teacher think it is a good idea for us to be exposed to Irish culture. This start already outside the pub when we see a man at the side passage making his waters on the wall. Our teacher say the customary Irish howya and the man turn around suddenly to answer. Mercedes nearly faint and then start laughing when I try to cover her eyes.

Did I tell you Mercedes was with us? When Conchubhair mention the cultural evening to her I am passing by in the corridor of the school so I say good idea we all go, the three of us. They look at each other and then say yes, good idea.

Conchubhair ask me have I not got to babysit, but I tell him that I am glad to say that Theo and Cleo are gone to their cousin's house. He ask did they take the car, but this is a joke.

The pubs here have very well-dressed doormen. They look like head-waiters in the restaurants of Madrid, except that their suits do not fit them so well because of the muscles. Their collars must be very tight because they are twitching their shoulders very much.

The pub is very full when we go in and I think they are giving away the drink free because everyone is fighting to get to the bar. If you tried to play the violin here, you would poke someone in the eye.

Conchubhair and Mercedes find two seats and sit down. He tell me it is my round. That means here you pay for all the drinks. He ask for Guinness and he say Mercedes will have a Harvey Wallbanger. I laugh because I think this is the name of a motor-bicycle but he say no, it's a real drink.

When I come back with the drinks he ask what took so long and I tell him about the oysters. He laugh and Mercedes laugh too. She has a lovely laugh, mama y papa. I know you would like her and maybe some day I ask her to visit Madrid.

I put my own drink on the table and stand beside them. It is a drink called Ballysomething. The barman tell me it will tell me a lot about the Irish people. I ask him what he mean and he say it is because they complain about paying a few pounds a year for water from the tap, but they will pay many pesetas for a bottle of the stuff just because it has a few bubbles in it.

I tell this to Conchubhair and Mercedes but I do not think they hear me. He is looking at her and whispering something and she is nodding. I go to find a stool so I can join them.

When I come back with the stool they are not at the table I think they have gone to the toilets. I will not tell you about the toilets, mama y papa, in case you are reading this letter with your breakfast.

So I sit there drinking my Ballysomething and then I go back to the bar and ask for another one. But I must not say it right because this time he give me a creamy drink called Baileysomething. It is very nice and after I drink one I soon have two more. I wonder where my friends are gone but not as much as before.

Then a man at the next table lean over and ask me to I want any E. I say E? He say shh, yes, E. Then he wink and say ecstasy, and nod at the door of the caballero's toilet. I do not know what he mean and say no thanks I wait here for my two friends. He then say a strange thing. He say they are gone to a bordello.

I say I know this not true because there are no such places in Ireland. But he say it is called Lillie's and it is famous. Bono and Van the Man go there, he tell me. And all the film stars when they are in town. I tell him I am shocked to hear such a thing, that I learn at school that Ireland is a Catholic country like Spain.

I get up and start to look around the pub for Mercedes. Jwhen I stand up I have to sit down again quickly as the place start to spin. The Baileysomething drink is stronger than milk, I think. When I walk I bang into a lot of people and say sorry, sorry.

Then I come to a door with 'guns' written on the glass. But it is backwards I think. I open the door and look inside. There is a very, very small room like the place jwhere the maid keeps the brooms at home. There is a table and two chairs.

And jwho is sitting on them, mama y papa?

It is Mr McClancy and his friend. His friend is the woman I meet jwhen I arrive first at McClancy house. Now she jump up very quickly and grab some papers off the table.

Mr McClancy also jump up and shout Haysoos.

She tell him not to swear but I say that is my name. She laugh and say fancy meeting you here. But Mr McClancy is shouting it not funny at all. What will people think? Then she say what about me, this a funny place you pick for a private meeting. Yes, he say, but I think nobody see us here.

Well, she say, we have to come to some other arrangement. Mr McClancy cough and tell me this is, ah, Ms Wilde, a business colleague. Then he open his wallet and give me twenty pounds. I have decided you deserve a raise, he say.

Ms Wilde pick up her bag and walk out very quickly. I tell Mr McClancy I am looking for Conchubhair, but he is not listening. He want to run after Ms Wilde.

But first he run back and say I must tell nobody about this meeting, because it is all very delicate. I say okay, I only tell my English class, but he grab my collar and shout, are you mad, I said nobody and I mean nobody. I nod my head and then he run out. Nodding my head make me feel dizzy so I get some more of the creamy drink.

I do not remember much about jwhat happen next. I think I try to find the bordello and someone in the street show me the way. But it is very dark and all I can see is that I am in some kind of square or plaza and there are some broken steps down from the footpath. Then I remember, this is the place I see on the day I arrive from the airport. I nearly fall down the steps. Then I am knocking at the door but nobody comes. Then I kick it. Bono, I shout. Van the Man? Are you in there?

Then a huge man open the door suddenly and ask who am I. I tell him I am Jésus.

That is jwhen everything go black.

When I wake up I am in a taxi and nearly jhome at the McClancys. The taximan look back at me when I wake up and he say Haysoos. It is the same one I get from the airport.

I see you're settling in, he say.

Chapter 9

Merry Christmas, mama y papa!

Already I am jhere more than a month, but Irlanda is still being a very strange place. First, everybody go running around the shops many times and getting very tired and very cross. That is jwhy everybody fall asleep for a week after Christmas, and nobody go back to work.

Also they are jhaving a terrible custom called the Christmas Day Swimming.

I find out about this jwhen Mr McClancy is saying hurry up and finish your breakfast we are going to the Forty Foot. I say to him that he mean the Forty Feet, but he say I am right but also I am wrong. Mrs McClancy is not having the breakfast because she is still in bed. She have a late night out on the tiles, Mr McClancy tell me. I am wondering if she is being up on the roof, but he say no but she jhave come home flying.

Then Theo and Cleo come in crying and say maybe she crash into Santa Claus on the way and that is why he not come to their house. That is when Mr McClancy is nearly biting his cup, mama y papa, but then he say no hold on, he have seen Santa Claus himself last night, but he jhave been very tired and not able to carry his big sack up the stairs. That is why he hide the presents for Theo and Cleo under the stairs.

They run there and throw everything out but are not finding anything. They are making so much noise that Mrs McClancy come running down the stairs holding her jhead in her jhands. Jwhat are you doing, she shout at Theo and Cleo, and when they tell her about Santa Claus not coming she say, don't be silly, he have left the things in the garden shed.

Mr McClancy say, oh yes, that is right, he remember now that she tell Santa Claus not to be stupid putting things under the stairs where everybody fall over them. He say Santa Claus hurt his back bringing them out to the shed in the dark when he fall over a cat.

Theo and Cleo not hear this because they are running out to the shed. Then I see them going very fast past the window because Santa Claus have been bringing them the mountain bikes. They are going up the road very fast. Mr McClancy is opening the front door and shouting for them to come back because they are wearing only the pyjamas. But when they come back they are walking and crying again because, mama y papa, they crash the bikes into each other!

Mr McClancy tell them to stop balling, but they are saying the mountain bikes are a right off. He say they only get a scratch and a broken spokes, but Theo say it ruin his Christmas. Anyway, he say, he really want a Hardly Davison. Cleo say she want a Hardly Davison, too, but Mr McClancy say here, here and give them some money. Theo say that not enough to buy a Hardly Davison but when Mr McClancy say okay, give it back, Theo say maybe he save it up.

The paper moneys jhere are funny, mama y papa, they have pictures of El Bert on them. Conchubhair say it is because he have been Minister for Finance. Maybe now they have to change it because they get a new Government.

After the breakfast, Mr McClancy's friend Fred is blowing his horn outside the door. Mr McClancy throw me a towel and say, come on, we are going swimming. I say but I have not bringing my swimming suit with me, because everybody tell me the water in Irlanda is very cold. But he say nonsense, you won't need any, and you'll soon warm up wait and see.

Fred say, that's right Haysoos, it will be an experience.

Then he say here take a swig from this and he give me a very big bottle with brandy in it. But I tell him I not like it, thank you.

Jwell, mama y papa, when we get to the place they call the Forty Foot, it is full of big fat men who have also been forgetting their swimming suits! I am glad there are not being any women jhere because they not know where to look if they come for a swim. Mr McClancy say oh yes, the ladies wanted to come jhere but we made it too hot for them.

I am getting out of my clothes behind the towel but I am still thinking about how hot is the water. Then Fred shout quick, here's the women, and I jump in very quickly.

They have being making a joke about the water being hot, mama y papa! I think I turn into a block of ice. I am trying to remember the word for help, but even when I remember it I am not able to say it. I just scream instead and they understand me anyway.

Someone is throwing me a red-and-white ring which hit me on the head. I forget what happen next until I wake up with the crowd around me. A man is saying I am a very strange colour and I say I am from Madrid, but he say he have being to Madrid and never see purple people there. Mr McClancy and Fred are saying okay, okay, back off, and putting their towels around me. Fred say am I sure I not jhave a swig. It taste very nice this time.

I am warm jwhen we get back to the house and Mr McClancy tell me to stop singing. Then I go to bed. When I get up again I go downstairs and I am too late for the dinner. But I find much food on the table because they have not been eating all the turkey and ham. Also the plum pudding which have no plums in it. I am heating all this in the microwave, and then I sit down and think of my family in Madrid and my grandmother's ranch where they know how to enjoy Christmas.

Where are the McClancys? They are asleep in front of the television which is having a religious programme on it.

It is called *Glenroe* and everybody there is all the time saying Jwell Holy God!

Chapter 10

January

Ola!

Mrs McClancy and her friends are having been talking about the nuns again today (you see I am learning my tensions).

She have having another meeting and jwhen I bring in the tea and biscuits they stop talking for a minute. Mrs Lemming go ahem ahem. I think she jhave a frug in her throat like they say jhere. But then she ask Mrs McClancy do I understand English. I am nodding and saying *si*, but Mrs McClancy say about as much as you speak Irish and they all laugh.

Then they forget about me I think. I listen to them talking and it remind me of my grandfather talking about the old days jwhen El Generalissimo was planning his great battles.

Bunny – that is what the other women call Mrs McClancy – Bunny is saying we must jhave a plan of action to outflank the enemy. She take out a big map and put it on the coffee table. It nearly spill the tea. She stab at it with her finger and nearly make a hole in it because she have very long nails.

The main thing, she say, is that the open space must be having been saved for the people, and the old jhouse of the nuns like wise. She say it is full of history, and the man called Cedric say no, it should be her story with all those good sisters. They all laugh except Bunny who say, be serious.

She say she have written to the Minister for Something and Something and Something about making the big jhouse an interpretative centre. I do not know why they want to do this because I learn that big word at school – Conchubhair say it mean a huge car park and half-finished toilets.

Anyway, Bunny, I mean Mrs McClancy, say she also is writing to the President about it.

The man called Cedric say she will understand, because she likes living in a big house herself, with lots of open space around it.

Mrs Young then say yes, I don't think she would like of cheap jhouses were built right up to the walls of the Aras like they want to do jhere.

Mrs McClancy say she have nothing against cheap jhouses but in their right place. If they build them jhere we will all soon be living in cheap houses. But then she say quickly, of course that not the real reason for this committee – what she and all of them want is to jhave a nice open space.

With a big high fence around it, say Mrs Young.

Mrs Mc C ask then if anyone know anything about the old house's history. Ms Mimble, who say nothing before this, then tell them someone tell jher that someone called the Big Fellow often stay there.

Cedric say that must jhave been fun for the nuns.

Ms Mimble say no, the nuns did not live there then. It was Lady Something.

Mrs McClancy say, good lord jhow did he manage to fight the Brits at all, and Cedric say was there such a thing as a safe house at all with the Big Fellow around.

Then they talk about money. We will need plenty of it, say Mrs Young. I think they jhave plenty already, but Mrs McClancy say don't worry, she is organising a fashion show.

Mrs Young say, with clothes from your own shop, Bunny? Mrs McClancy say yes. Mrs Young say, but we want people to come, and Cedric start making noise like a cat.

But Mrs McClancy say she have it all organised. She was talking already to Norma and Margaret and they are having told her they will take lots of tickets for their friends. And she is inviting Gay and Kay.

Cedric say if she get Kay to compare, then Gay will give them a big plug on the radio. I look at the radio, but it have batteries only.

Mrs McClancy say no, she want Pat Kenny, and Cedric say don't we all.

Mrs Young say jwhat about the models, and Mrs McClancy say she hope to get Naomi. Mrs Young say you must be joking she not get out of bed for less than ten thousand pounds, but Mrs McClancy say she pull a few strings. Ms Mimble say suddenly that is jwhat she wear most of the time and they all laugh.

Yes Bunny, say Cedric, you will jhave to keep your husband away that night.

They all laugh again, but not Bunny.

Then they see me standing there and say maybe I could be a model for the night. I go red and say no thank you very much, but Cedric say yes, he can see me in a suit of lights. I wonder why he keep talking about electricity?

Chapter 11

Ola mama y papa!

Today I learn a new Irish English word, mama y papa. It is mortified. It have something to do with toilets and floors, and it happen to Mrs McClancy.

The trouble start jwhen Mrs and Mrs McClancy go out for the evening to a party at their friend's house. They get dressed up, especially Mrs McClancy who try on five different dresses before they go. Mr McClancy stand at front door rattling his keys and shouting up the stairs. She keep coming out on the stairs and asking jwhat about this one and he keep saying fine, fine, and then she go back in agan and put on another dress.

He ask her has she got the whole boutique up there with her. She say it is an important party because she want to make a good impression on the VIPs. Some of them are the parents of the school friends of Theo and Cleo and they could be useful. Mr McClancy say can she not just go and enjoy herself, and she say oh yes she know jwhat he mean by that.

He then ask her what she mean by saying she know what he mean by that, and she answer that she mean he drink too much Black Hedge and then bore the burro off someone in a corner for the night. He say what about her – one gin and tonic and she think she is a chair. Or maybe he mean Cher.

She say that ridiculous because Cher has more lifts than the Empire State Building but she is not needing anything like that. But she say she will be doing the aerobics when the new leisure and crafts centre open. The nuns used to worry about our souls, she say, but when they go we look after our bodies instead.

Mr McClancy say, well if you don't who will?

They go out to the party and tell me to make sure Theo and Cleo go to bed at proper time. I say yes of course. Theo and Cleo are in their bedrooms already, but they are not asleep, they are doing their homework for school. They get a lot of homework in Ireland, because I think they spend too much time in their rooms (except of course when they get out the window like the time they go for a joyride).

But now I look into their rooms quietly and they are both busy at doing their homework. Theo is at his computer, and jwhen I look in first I think I see very strange pictures on it, but they vanish when I come into the room. Theo jump and ask what am I sneaking around for. I tell him I am not sneaking, that I am in charge like his mother and father say. I ask him what he study on the computer and he tell me he is using the Internet to find out about strange customs in faraway countries. I say they were strange pictures of a man and a woman, but he say I imagine them, he is learning about gorillas.

Then I peep into Cleo's room but she is using the telephone and I go away. She is listening not talking. Later, I go to the phone downstairs because I want to ask Mercedes to come to the pictures with me, but I hear Cleo is still using the phone. It is only making very strange noises like someone who has been running for a long time and someone else shouting yes, yes a lot. I say who is there and all the noises stop suddenly.

I usc the phone myself then to call Mercedes and a man in the jhouse answer. He ask is the job oxo.

I say no, this is Jésus, and he tell me to cop myself on and stop messing, the stuff is on the way from Rosslare to the usual. I tell him I do not know where this Rosslare is and I just want Mercedes. He say he tell me before that flashy cars are out. Stick to the Jap imports and keep the heat off our backs. As you can see, mama y papa, the English language is much more difficult than what I learn at school. Sometimes I think maybe I should have studied Swahili instead.

Anyway, I tell this man that I am not looking for a car, that I am looking for a girl. He say, listen pal, you are pushing your look. Then he say oh Haysoos, you mean the Spanish Mercedes. He call her to the phone and she say, hello Conchubhair. I say no it's Jésus, and she say, oh sorry. I ask her to come to the pictures with me tomorrow but she say she is washing her hair. Mercedes have very clean hair, mama y papa, because whenever I phone her she is washing it.

I am putting down the phone when I get a surprise. It is Mr and Mrs McClancy coming home early from the party. They come in the door and bang it with a very loud bang. I nearly drop the phone. Mrs McClancy say I jhope you not phoning Madrid again, our phone bill is gone through the roof.

Never mind that, say Mr McClancy, where Theo and Cleo? I ask him was there not enough Black Hedge at the party and he say what, what? Mrs McClancy say she never so mortified in all her life. I ask what is mortified and she say she wanted the floor to open up and swallow her. First the roof and now the floor – I look up and down but see no holes.

Then Mr McClancy shout for Theo and Cleo to come down. They come down slowly, yawning and saying they have been being asleep. Mrs McClancy scream at them then. Why, she ask them, did you put Derek Derrigan's head down in the toilet today?

Theo say because he was not in school yesterday. Mr McC say one more crack like that and he will wipe his smile from his face. Theo say he will phone Childline. Mrs McClancy say shut up, she was never so mortified in all her life as when Dr Derrigan came up to her and ask is she Theo's mother. And to think, she said, that we pay huge fees to that school so you meet the right people.

Then Cleo say it all Dirty Derrigan's fault, he say bad things about Mr McClancy. What things, ask Mrs McClancy, and Cleo say he said that Mr McClancy have a mistress.

Mr McClancy shout that it not true. She is not a teacher, he shout, then he say I mean she is a business colleague.

That is when Mrs McClancy hit him with the small coffee table.

I go to bed then.

Chapter 12

Ola!

Something very strange happen today, mama y papa. I am coming down the stairs in the morning to start making the breakfast jwhen I hear Mr McClancy talking on the phone. At first I think he is talking about me because he say my name a lot. But then I hear him say, are you sure Ashling? That is the name of their daughter in America, I told you I am staying in her room.

Then I hear Mr McClancy say my name again and saying are you sure? Then he shout and say five months and who is the father? Then he say are you sure again, and he say, no of course I do not mean that. Then he shout, he's what? Then he say he is not shouting, but how the hell did she get mixed up with a rap singer?

Then he say no of course I won't tell her yet. Then he put the phone down and stand there shaking his jhead. Then he look and see me and say, I am too young to be a grandfather. Just then Mrs McClancy come down the stairs and ask who was on the phone. He say it was Ashling but she was in a hurry going to work.

Mrs McClancy ask jhim does he think she is mad, because it is four o'clock in the morning in Boston. Who was it really? she ask. Mr McClancy say it was really her and maybe he make a mistake about going to work. Maybe she say going to bed, he say, it was a bad line. But Mrs McClancy ask, why is she phoning at four o'clock in the morning, was it just for a chat, or was she looking for more money I suppose?

Mr McClancy nod and say yes that's it. She shake her head and say, how much is that you've sent her since she went over there to become a rock star? He say, not much, and she say, nonsense you always have been giving her too much. Then Mrs McClancy say is she still working in that awful Irish bar full of Provos after the education we gave her? He say no, she has joined a band. She say some awful Irish fiddle band no doubt, but Mr McClancy say no, it is something more ethnic than that.

Theo and Cleo are hearing this and start to shout will she be on MTV. They run into sitting room and switch on the television but it is only Zig and Zag as usual.

I forget I not tell you before about Zig and Zag. I think at first they are politicians. One day I hear Mr McClancy say that El Bert and El Bruton are like Zig and Zag because it is El Dic jwho is pulling the strings and making them jump.

Then Mrs McClancy say that is not how they work, that you have to put your hand up in their backs like a glove. Mr McClancy say that exactly jwhat he mean and she say don't be vulgar in front of the children. But the children not listening because they jhave their Walkmans on jwhen they are jhaving their dinner.

Later I jhear Mr McClancy on the phone again. I think at first he is talking to their daughter again because he is saying calm down, nobody knows. Then he say don't worry the job is oxo.

He say a lot more things I do not understand, about stroking the moneymen and juggling many balls in the air, but he would look after her.

Then he ask how is she getting on with the Councillor. He jhope she is looking after jhim very well. I think he is talking to Ms Wilde, mama y papa, and now I think maybe she is a nurse. She is minding this Councillor, who is not well, I think, because Mr McClancy laugh suddenly and say I can't wait till he gets the video in the post, that should make him sit up.

Chapter 13

Ola!

I am going to be a film star, mama y papa! They are making the films all over Ireland. It can be very dangerous, because everywhere you go you might be bumping into some people dressed in funny clothes and shining bright lights and cameras and shouting cut. And it is the same man who is making all the films, mama y papa!

I think he is a famous film-making man from Hollywood, because jwhen his picture is in the paper shaking hands with the actor called Hugh Grant, Mrs McClancy is saying, oh now there is someone I wish I could meet, and Mr McClancy say do you mean Cecil Dee Higgins?

She say of course not, I mean I'd like to get my hands on Hugh Grant, and he say she sound like a farmer because all they ever want is a huge grant, too. Then he laugh to himself. Sometimes I do not understand jwhat the Irish people are laughing at.

I ask Conchubhair our teacher who is Cecil Dee Higgins, and he say he think I know who you mean. He say he is not a famous film producer, but is a leprechaun from Galway! I tell him I do not believe jhim, that I hear about these leprechauns in our folklore studies and that they are not real people. Conchubhair say yes, but did you learn then that they live at the end of a rainbow and always have a crock of gold? I say yes, I remember something like that, and he say well nobody else can get their hands on millions of pounds as easily as Cecil Dee. He is really magic, say Conchubhair, because he use the money for building castles in the air.

But Conchubhair then say he is not knocking the castle because he hope some day himself to go and work in it. But first he must go and learn jhow to play the card-game correctly.

But jwhat do you think happen the same day, mama y papa? I am walking with Mercedes in the middle of Dublin when we come around a corner and see a robbing happening before our ears! There is a car stopped at the traffic lights and I see two boys throwing a brick through the window. Then they open the door and take out a bag and start to run away. There is a lady in the car and she is screaming and screaming, but nobody is coming to jhelp jher. Mercedes say, do something, and of course I run after the two boys shouting stop stop.

They run very fast, but I run faster, and I catch one of them and knock him down at the corner. He shout help help, but I bang his head off the ground and run after the other one who have the bag. He is also screaming, help help, but I trip him up also and take the bag and sit on him till the police come.

But the police do not come. Instead a whole lot of men and some women come running down the road and shout at me what the hell I think I am doing. I tell them I catch these robbers of the lady in the car. Then I look around and see cameras and bright lights all shining on me. They shout at me that they are making a film. I do not believe them. But when I look up the road and see the man called Cecil Dee standing there I know it is true.

I get up slowly and say sorry sorry to everybody, especially the child who I squash on the road. Then I look again and see that it is not a boy but a girl with a very dirty face. She say, get off me, you Spanish gobshite. I do not know how she know I am from Spain.

Some people with other cameras start to take pictures of me. One of them ask me my name but when it is in the paper the next day they call me José Maria like the golfer.

Somebody is saying call the police and arrest this hooligan, but Cecil Dee hold up his hands and say he never enjoy anything so much since the day he meet Fidel. I want to ask him how does he know my uncle, but then I think maybe it is some other Fidel. Then he say well he must be off because he is really visiting another film around the corner and just stopped the car because this one looked more exciting. Everybody laugh then and he drive off.

Then I look at the girl and boy again, and what do you think, mama y papa, it is Theo and Cleo. Then I remember I hear Mrs McClancy saying she know somebody who is looking for two nice children to be in a film. She say this to Theo and Cleo when they are having breakfast. They say they are not going to be in any stupid film and ask their mother does she think they are Billy Barry's children. I think this is a very strange thing to ask, because of course they are Mr McClancy's children.

But Mrs McClancy just laugh and then mention money to them. They say that is not what Macaulay Culkin get, but she say you have to start somewhere and maybe next year they get what he get. Anyway, she say, she promise her friend to send them quickly because some other children drop out with the flu (it is not the same word as a chimney after all).

She say her friend is in a hurry. She have a funny name, I think. Mr McClancy say she is Mrs Twenty-percent. He hope they know what they are doing, but Mrs McClancy say look at that nice Hugh O'Conor, he did very well. All she know is the film is about crime in Dublin and they need them today. Her friend Mrs Twentypercent tell her they are perfect for the film.

Mrs McClancy say she not know who is the star, but maybe it will be Gabriel Byrne or even Hugh Grant. She hope to find out later so that she can be introduced. Maybe I can rope him in for one of our drives, she say.

Mr McClancy say she talk like someone in a cowboy film, and she say he should know all about that.

After Cecil Dee drive off, they let me go and I come back to find Mercedes. I think she is crying because she is leaning on the wall with her head in her hands and her shoulders are shaking. But when she look up she have tears in her eyes but she is laughing and laughing. But then, mama y papa, she say I am better than Arnold Schwarzenegger!

I hope they will leave my part in the film so that you can see it when it gets to Madrid.

It have a strange name.

Crimeline.

Chapter 14

Ola!

Yesterday, mama y papa, I am going to the famous Lansdowne Road to see the Irish football team play the English football team. It is a friendly game, they tell me before I go. This is why I do not think I am learning much English at all sometimes, because everything jhere means the other way around. It is like jwhen you go to Australia and the water goes out of the bath the other way.

Another thing strange is that the Irish team is English. The two teams all fly in from England, and jwhen they talk on the television, I think they all sound the same.

Mr McClancy is having the tickets for the game. He tell us at breakfast. I ask him if he is a big fan for many years, but he laugh and say of course not, they are corporate.

I ask Conchubhair later what that word means and he say it is special catfood. I do not understand but he say, oh yes, if it is corporate it is only for the fat cats. He then tell the class an old Irish story about a man called Ordinary Joe Soap who spend all his money following the football team when nobody else would. He stuck with them, say Conchubhair, through thick and thin, even through the Bad Old Days of Owing Hand & The Like.

But now, he say, with tears in his eye, the sun is shining, but poor Ordinary Joe Soap is left out in the rain, while someone called Johnny Come Lately is inside there eating all the smoked salmon, and not knowing their Alps from their Ebro.

I say to jhim that the sun is not shining all the time now, and Conchubhair say what do I mean. I say what about the time Spain win three-one. He go very quiet then.

Anyway, mama y papa, I was telling you about the breakfast time. Mr McClancy get a big surprise jwhen Mrs McClancy say suddenly that she want to go to the game. He say since jwhen were you interested in soccer? She say yes she know she would not be seen within a burro's roar of Lansdowne Road unless it was the rugby football (I tell you all about that strange game some other time, mama y papa).

So why in the name of Haysoos, ask Mr McClancy, do you want to go now?

She say it is because she hear the team often detonate their balls.

Or maybe it is donate.

Mr McClancy tell her she have a fat chance, she is not knowing any of the team, but Mrs McClancy say she have met Paul McGrath once at a charity lunch and he was very nice man. But a bit big for a scrum half, she say.

Theo and Cleo start shouting ooh, aah, and I think they have spilled hot tea on themselves, but Mr McClancy shout shut up and they stop.

Mrs McClancy also say she hear that Mr Charlton is a very kind man, and maybe she will be able to persuade him to come to one of her little events.

Oh yes, say Mr McClancy, he turn up at the opening of an envelope if there is enough money in it. (So would I, mama y papa – will you be sending one soon?) He say he cannot turn on the radio without hearing Saint Jack selling tinned salmon, yogurt and cars.

I forget to tell you, mama y papa, who this Saint Jack is. He is the manager of the Irish football team. He is a very big man who do not speak English at all, I think. He come from a place called Geordieland.

47

Conchubhair tell the class that the peasants have throwing out their ancient pictures of Pope Jack and President Jack to make space for Saint Jack. Mercedes say that her family on the Northside are not peasants, she think, because they only have pictures of Pamela Anderson. No, wait, she say, they also have pictures of a woman called Nora, but it is on a dartboard.

But before I go to the class yesterday, Mrs McClancy is asking Mr McClancy who was he keeping the extra ticket for, and he say oh, a client, but he will phone a friend to get more. Someone who owe him a favour, he say.

Anyway, mama y papa, to cut a long story brief, he get tickets for all of the family and me, too. They are special tickets and we are in a very nice room in the stand with windows to see the game, and everybody is standing around with drinks. Everybody in the room, I mean, not the ordinary people outside, who are not drinking, I think.

I look out to see if I can see Ordinary Joe Soap, but all I see is some happy people and some other people across the field who do not look happy. Maybe they are the friends of Joe Soap, I do not know.

Mr McClancy is at one side of room talking to some men and some women. I think one of them is Ms Wilde but maybe not because she look different and wear a dark suit and have her hair different. Mrs McClancy is talking to some men in blazers and asking them about their balls, maybe.

She say she would like one signed by all fifteen of the team. They say you mean eleven, and she say oh no, they are not a cricket team and laugh. The men do not laugh. She ask how many of the team went to Belvedere like her friend Tony, then they laugh.

I am drinking one of those nice Ballysomething or Baileysomething drinks, jwhen I look around but can not see Theo or Cleo anywhere. Maybe they are going to the toilets, I think. I look for them everywhere, but they are

48

not there. But then the national anthem start and I forget about them.

They have a funny national anthem here, mama y papa. It is in the Irish language. Conchubhair say everybody can sing it but only some peoples know what it all mean. He say it is all about shooting and dying, but he also say that some of the words mean that helpers have come from over the sea, so maybe it is right for the Irish team. They are the only people who do not know the words.

The game start then, and it is very short. Ireland score a goal, and I am looking for Theo and Cleo. I think I see them in the crowd far across the other side of the field and am just going to tell Mrs McClancy when the riot start. Mama y papa, it is terrible! The English fans are breaking up seats and throwing them down on the Irish and many people are hurt.

Everybody is running away, and I think I see Theo and Cleo running with them. Then everybody is gone but the English fans are still there. They are quiet now, but the police are hitting and hitting them just to be sure.

Then Mrs McClancy start screaming where are Theo and Cleo. I say they are out there. Mr McClancy come running over shouting what do you mean, and I tell him they go out before the game start. *Madre de dio*, he say, and run out of the room. Mrs McClancy run, too. I think maybe they love their children after all. I look over at the woman I think is Ms Wilde. She wink at me, and then say something strange – how is the black male going? I tell her I have never met any of the team.

Then I run out to follow the McClancys. Phew, mama y papa, everything is okay! They find Theo and Cleo talking to a nice policeman. Theo is asking him can he borrow his baton to help with the hitting of the English fans, but the policeman say to Mr and Mrs McClancy, please take them home before they cause more trouble.

Mrs McClancy say what do you mean, and he point to the backs of their tee-shirts, which they are wearing under their anoraks. Theo's tee-shirt has one word on it, the Irish word 'Gobshite' in very big writing. But I do not understand the three words on Cleo's shirt at all: 'Gazza Is A'.

How could that cause trouble, I ask Mr McClancy, but he just say shut up and let us get out of here before they deport us all.

This morning they read the papers about the football game and all the fighting. Mr McClancy say well at least nobody is blaming us.

Then Mrs McClancy say, is that your client? She show him a picture in the paper. It is Mr McClancy talking to the woman I think is Ms Wilde.

Who? Her? he ask. Then he shake his head and say no, I do not know who she is. She was just there, he say.

I am saying nothing, and later Mr McClancy give me more paper money with the picture of El Bert.

Chapter 15

Ola!

My hand is shaking when I start this letter, mama y papa. There have been another meeting of Mrs McClancy's committee and they are saying about how the area is having being invaded by fly-by-nights and bloodsuckers. Maybe I come home straight away.

These fly-by-nights are having been seen, say Mrs McClancy, up at the convent talking to the Mother Superior.

The man called Cedric say she is an old bat.

Yes, say Mrs Lemming, but she is not batty.

Mrs McClancy say she hear that someone is trying to have the place rezoned.

Ms Mimble suddenly say there was never any rezoning with that one and laugh to herself.

Cedric say never mind all this talk about rezone – what he want to know is what about Boyzone. They ask him what he mean and he say they should be in the fashion show.

Mrs McClancy say she hear they are all from the Northside, but she look into it.

This Boyzone, mama y papa, are a singing group. They sing for the teeny-boppers, which is people who are age five or six. Theo and Cleo say they would not be seen dead at one of their concerts. But I think this is some kind of joke because I watch the television next time and of course there is nobody dead at the concert.

But I am telling you about the committee, where again

I am bringing in the tea and biscuits. They are saying they will have to find out who are behind the fly-by-nights or we will all be swamped.

Mrs Young say she hear that it is touch and go with the Council. I think this is some kind of game they play, mama y papa. Yes, say Cedric, he have been making phone calls but they keep passing the book.

Mrs McClancy say she will try to find out more about their little game, because it look like it getting dirty.

Mrs Young ask what about your husband, and Mrs McClancy say, what about him? Mrs Young say he have his ear to the ground. I think this is very strange thing to say, because Mr McClancy have ears like you and me.

But maybe that is not what she mean, because Mrs McClancy just say no, she have been asking him if his building friends know anything and he have been saying no, he too busy with other interests.

Then the phone ring and she go to answer it.

Mrs Young say oh of course, yes, Cheltenham is coming up soon. And Cedric say I hear he has his eye on a certain filly. Mrs Young say it more than his eye. Then they both laugh and Mrs McClancy come back in and ask what the big joke.

Mrs Lemming say she not understand what so funny about horses anyway. Mrs McClancy say, oh horses, don't talk to me about horses. She say her husband have joined something called a consortium which own a horse.

Cedric ask which piece he own, and Mrs Young start to rattle her cup on her saucer so that I have to catch it in case it fall on the carpet.

Ms Mimble ask what the name of the horse, but Mrs McClancy is not sure, she think she hear him say it is called Bigfellow. Ms Mimble say she never heard of it but she ask her horsey friends. I think she is a very strange woman if she think horses can talk, mama y papa!

Mrs Young ask then if Councillor Clodd also own this horse, because she have seen him sitting in car talking to Mr McClancy.

She say she think they have strange looks on their faces. (Maybe they afraid of the fly-by-nights?)

Mrs McClancy say she find out about that, but she have news for them about the President's visit to the nuns. It will be later this year, she say, and there will be a big splash.

Cedric say he hope they not throw Mary in the duckpond. Mrs McClancy say she hope to meet the President when she come. Mrs Lemming ask did she get an invitation, but she say no, she is writing on behalf of the committee. She is telling the President all about their little movement to preserve the open spaces.

Then she say she is also getting help from someone who used to meet Mary a lot when she was at the bar.

I did not know Mrs Robinson go to pubs. I hope it not the same one I visit.

Cedric say Mrs McClancy have a better chance if she call herself Mrs Connors and live in a caravan, but Mrs Lemming suddenly say she have enough and is going home. Ms Mimble say yes, she also is fed up (they only have two biscuits).

Everybody start talking very loud then, until Cedric say sorry about something and they all sit down again.

Mrs Young then ask about the fashion show. Mrs McClancy say she have hired a big hotel in town because it have a swimming pool. She say if they have a bridge over it, and have the models on the bridge, it get pictures in the paper.

But what about Naomi, they ask her. She say, what about Naomi? Mrs Young say, you said you could get her. Oh, say Mrs McClancy, yes, she have been talking to her agent but Naomi is being busy that night.

Washing her hair no doubt, say Mrs Young.

But Cedric say no, that is the night she write her next book.

Chapter 16

¡Ola!

I have at last visited the Northside, mama y papa. It was an accident.

What happen is, I am going into town with Theo and Cleo because they are getting tickets for Bon Jovi. We go on the Dart – that is what they call the electric train. Theo say they have one in Frankfurt as well but it start with another letter. Then he make funny noises with his mouth and Cleo laugh until she slide under table.

I have not being on the Dart before, but the station is not far from the McClancy house. But the platform is crowded and when the Dart train is arriving I get into one carriage but when I look around, Theo and Cleo are not in it, too. They must have being pushed into other carriage. I go looking for them at the next station, but they are not in the next carriage either.

What happen next is that I am still looking for them in all the carriages when the Dart go right through the middle of the town and I do not look out the window in time. Everything changes and then I know I have travelled to the Northside. There are many buggies and babies suddenly getting into my carriage, and we go through a deep valley where the shopping trolleys are growing on the slopes.

I am looking out the window of my carriage when we come to a station and I see some apartments. Mama y papa, I think they are the apartments from *Los Commitments*! I am looking at them and wondering if

maybe this one is where the horse live on the top floor when suddenly I see Theo and Cleo going out of the gate.

I jump out and run after them, and I shout but they do not hear me. They are going to some big shops in a shopping centro and I follow them. Maybe this is another place where they get Bon Jovi tickets, but I do not know.

When I am at the shops I suddenly hear much screaming and shouting from inside. A man is attacking Theo. He have catching him by the collar of his anorak and shaking him, but then I see Cleo coming very quickly with a trolley and she crash into the man. He shout and hold his knee, and let Theo go. I call them, but they run away very fast.

That is when I get lost in the Northside. I am afraid at first, mama y papa, because of all the terrible stories Conchubhair is telling about this place. But I walk for a long time, looking for the children, and everybody is very friendly. I look carefully when I am crossing the roads, but I see no joyriders or galloping horses.

I am beginning to think all of the stories are a lie, but then I see some men sitting in a car watching a house. I ask them what is the way to the Dart, but they say go away, we are busy. They are very rough men, I think, and very rude, not like other people I meet here. I think they are some kind of gang, maybe even buglers who are going to bugle the house they are watching.

But what do you think happen next, mama y papa? The door of the house open and Mercedes walk out! I run up to her and shout about the men in the car. I tell this to a man who is closing the door of the house – I point to the car down the road and tell him I think they are buglers coming to bugle his house. He say nothing, he just bang the door suddenly.

I am standing there with Mercedes and I am going to say to her that this man is having bad manners, but just then I see the man again running out the back of the house and jumping over the wall into another house.

Maybe he is going for the police, I think, but just then I hear shouting very loud behind me and the buglers come running up the road.

One of them run after the man, but the other one catch my arm and start shouting my name at me and asking what I think I am doing? Mercedes start to explain, and she talk very fast. But I do not know what she is saying, because it not English and not Spanish. It is Euskadi.

I tell the man she is a Basque, but he shout that I am another, and he tell me I am under a rest. Then he take out a badge and show it to me and say he taking me to the station. I tell him no thank you, I not want to go on Dart until I find Theo and Cleo. But he just say get into the car.

It is not the Dart station at all, mama y papa, but the police station! They bring me into a room and ask me a lot of questions about where I hide the lute. I tell them I am from Spain and they say yes they know about the Costa del Crime. I hear of many costas but never that one. I tell them I am looking for Theo and Cleo but they do not believe me.

Then another car stop at the police station and a policewoman bring in Theo and Cleo. They empty their pockets and many things from the shop fall on desk. They are crying and saying it all a mistake.

The sergeant say you can say that again.

Then they see me and ask me to help.

The sergeant say, you know them?

Well, well, he say then, it look like we have the whole gang.

Chapter 17

Ola again!

I forget to tell you yesterday, mama y papa, that I get free again! I am safe at home again on the Southside. It was all a big cock-up, say Mr McClancy. The police phone him and he come running in his car.

At first he think it is just Theo and Cleo he have come for, and I think he get a surprise when he see me too.

Theo and Cleo might go to jail, but I am free, don't worry. The sergeant say I am in wrong place at wrong time. I say yes, it is Ireland, but nobody else enjoy my little joke.

The sergeant is asking Mr McClancy if he have any more foreign students staying with him, and say he have his sympathy. He say that last year he have two French ones and they live in the toilet.

I think this is not a very nice place to put them.

Mr McClancy ask the sergeant not to throw the book at Theo and Cleo. The sergeant say his hands are tied.

Mr McClancy then say that he is a personal friend of the Minister for Justice. The sergeant ask is that a fact, and he say, oh yes me and Máire go back a long way.

The sergeant say you mean Nora, and Mr McClancy say oh yes, he will be forgetting his own head next.

The sergeant say yes of course, it is very hard to keep up with Ministers for Justice the way they keep changing them. Then he say he suppose Mr McClancy is a personal friend of the Thorny General as well.

Mr McClancy say as a matter of fact he is, and the sergeant say very quickly which one?

This is not an easy question to answer, mama y papa, because now in Ireland there are many Thorny Generals. They are like the rabbits on grandmama's ranch – first they are having just two, but now every time you look around there is another one. El Bruton get rid of some of them when he come into power, but he soon get a new one of his own.

Everyone say the new Thorny General is the best man for the job. I think he have a very messy job, because Conchubhair say when he hear his name that there will be blood on the carpet and heads will roll, but he will find out where the bodies are buried. When I see the Thorny General on the television he is always walking with a very heavy bag and I think he have the heads in there.

But when I say this last week in the McClancy house, Mr McClancy laugh and say no, it is old footage. He say the Thorny General have been saving a good man's skin last year. Then I am very puzzled, mama y papa, maybe that is what is in the bag? I hope he not drop it, but I watch him every time he come on television and he make it safely to the door every time.

El Bruton also change the Minister for Justice when he come into power. It is a tradition in Ireland that the Minister for Justice is always a woman. This is because they have to clean up the streets. They all promise to do this when they get the job.

In the police station, Mr McClancy is talking again about Nora and saying to the sergeant, did he know she is a great-grandniece of the Big Fellow? He say that he have been in her office and did the sergeant know she have a little statue of him there? The sergeant say yes he have seeing it himself on the television. Mr McClancy say no, it is on a desk.

Then he ask the sergeant if by any chance he know his friend the Super. I think at first he have gone mad and believe in Superman, but the sergeant is asking which Super is that now? Mr McClancy say O'Larrigan. The sergeant say that is amazing, that Mr McClancy know his uncle. He say he hope to see him on Sunday and will tell him Mr McClancy was requesting him.

Mr McClancy say oh it is a while since they met. The sergeant say where did they meet, and he say, at the golf club. The sergeant say that is funny because he know his uncle Seamus hate golf.

Mr McClancy say it must be some other Super then. Then he start to cry.

He tell the sergeant he have done his best, he want to bring up the children the way his father bring him up. He walk with bear feet to school in the winter, he say, and carry a sod of turf for the teacher's fire. The sergeant ask did it not burn him, but Mr McClancy is not hearing him. He say it is his wife's fault – she give them everything they want and now this happen.

The sergeant ask him what was the name of the school. Mr McClancy tell him it is Saint Mulacudda. The sergeant say he do not believe it, but Mr McClancy say it is true. The sergeant laugh and say no, he mean that his father go to the same school. Mr McClancy say, you do not mean Scratcher Savage the hurler?

The sergeant say the very one. Then they start laughing and talking about this thing called hurling. It sound very dangerous, mama y papa, and like the Thorny General's job it mean hitting people on the head very much. Mr McClancy is saying of course they all wear helmets now a daze, and the sergeant shout about some lady called Molly Coddles.

They are both laughing very loud. Then Mr McClancy is saying maybe this mean Theo and Cleo not have to see the judge. The sergeant say he will be seeing what he can do. Mr McClancy say he suppose the sergeant like a drop of the hard stuff, but the sergeant say that he like a Paddy himself. Off-duty, he say and laugh. Mr McClancy laugh louder and say it will be duty free.

When we get home he lock Theo and Cleo in their bedrooms. Then he start to call me some names which I think are very rude except I do not understand what they mean. When he stop for a breath I ask him how is his friend from the pub and he go purple in the face.

Just then Mrs McClancy come in and ask did we all have a nice day in town. I say yes thank you. She say she is glad we were not mugged because there is much of it about.

Mr McClancy make strange noise in his throat and say excuse me I have some work to do in my room.

Mrs McClancy say what kind of work at this hour and he say he will be busy pulling strings.

Chapter 18

March

Hello, mama y papa!

That is the word for ola here in Ireland. They also say it backwards sometimes so it sound like ohell. That is what Mr McClancy say on Sunday when Mrs McClancy's sister Birdie come to visit her.

I am getting a surprise when I open the front door because I think at first it is Mrs McClancy again! She look just the same as her but her clothes are more bright. And her hair is reminding me of the oranges that grow on grandmother's rancho. She look me up and down and say well, well, so you are the Spanish acquisition.

I ask Conchubhair what this word mean but he say it is about torturing people who do not believe everything the Catholic Church tell them to believe. He say the Spanish invented it but they still have it in Ireland. But it is now called a referendum.

I do not know why Mrs McClancy's sister Birdie call me a referendum, but she come in anyway and her sister come out into the hall and welcome her. They kiss each other on the cheeks and say Birdie and Bunny in very loud voices. That is when I hear Mr McClancy in the kitchen say hello backwards.

Then they look at each other and say, well how are you?

They tell each other that they are looking very well. Then Mrs McClancy's sister say, considering, and her sister stop smiling and say, considering what?

Oh nothing, say Birdie. Then she ask how is Mrs McClancy's daughter in America. Mrs McClancy say fine, fine, she have a good job and doing well. Birdie say no sign of her settling down over there? Mrs McClancy say, oh no, she think she stay there for a few years and then come home.

Her sister say oh really, but then she tell Mrs McClancy that she have some news about her own daughter Dervogilla. I think she say gorilla at first, but they have strange names here in Ireland, mama y papa, so I look in a book Conchubhair is having in the class. I also look for Wayne and Kylie (they are the names of some babies on the Dart) but they are not in the book. Conchubhair say they belong to a later stratum of culture. Now I have to find out what that mean, but that is how I am learning.

Mrs McClancy say oh and how is Dervogilla these days, is she studying for another degree or did she get any kind of a job yet? She say how expensive it is to keep them at college. Her sister say that is no problem the way she is fixed. I look closely at her but can not see where she was broken.

Then Birdie say that her daughter Dervogilla is getting married. Mrs McClancy say oh that is very sudden, but Birdie ask what she means by that?

Mrs McClancy say nothing, nothing, who is the lucky man? Her sister say he is a doctor. Mrs McClancy say she not ask what he do, she ask what his name. Oh it is Tom, say Birdie, Tom Thomson. Doctor Tom Thomson, she say then.

She meet him at a discussion group, say Birdie.

Well, say Bunny, she think for a minute she was going to say a disco. But of course Derv was never the disco type.

Don't call her that, say Birdie, it sound like a diesel oil.

Well, say Bunny, when is the big day? And Birdie say it is next month.

What is the big hurry, ask Bunny, and Birdie look at

her and say it is because they are going to the Third World then. I think at first they are going in a rocket, but then I remember that is what they call Africa and India here.

Bunny ask for how long, and Birdie say nine months or a year. Her sister say hmm. Then she say she know the doctor will be useful there but what will Derv do?

Her sister say again don't call her that. Then she say Dervogilla have degrees in psychology and philosophy, but she is also accordeon blue cook. Oh, say Bunny, that will be very useful, but Birdie say she also know all about new trission.

Then she say she want to invite everybody to the wedding. It will be a small one, she say. Oh, say Bunny. Yes, say Birdie, only two or three hundred guests. Oh, say Bunny again.

She say it a pity the McClancys' eldest daughter not able to come. Then she look at me and say bring José Maria too. Mrs McClancy tell her my name is Haysoos, and Birdie say that is the nearest you are being to religion.

But then her sister say maybe it not a good idea to bring him to her town because he is Spanish. Birdie say, oh that is all exaggerated. It is only the papers and the radio that are whipping it up, she say. Her husband Jim own five trawlers, she say, no six now, and some of his best friends are Spanish. Millionaires, she say then.

Then she ask how is Mr McClancy, and just then he come into the room. Birdie, he say in a loud voice, but I know he have hear her come in when he say hello backwards earlier. She ask him how are things in the building trade and he say you mean property development. Then he say it is up and down, up and down, just like the fishing boats, he suppose.

Birdie say oh the trawlers all have stabilisers now, but she hear it is much more rocky on land. Mr McClancy laugh and say he hope to make a big hall himself soon.

She say nothing fishy she hope. I think the hall is big enough.

They talk about the wedding again then, and I bring in some tea and cakes. Birdie ask did I bake the buns, but Bunny laugh and say oh no, they are fergles. Her sister say did you know his cousin is the Minister for Finance? I am going to tell her that no, my cousin is being in the Ministerio de Urbanizacion, but they are not talking about me, it is someone called Rooree. I do not know how they change the subject so quickly here in Ireland, mama y papa!

Mrs McClancy is saying she always shop in fergles. Mr McClancy say he hope she can afford it after his cousin's budget, because he used to be next door to a communist. Birdie say yes, but now he live in a different neighbour-hood all together. She say she hope they control the public spending. Mr McClancy ask her then how much is the wedding going to cost, but she just say they have to push out the boats.

When she is gone I ask Mrs McClancy is Birdie her twin. Oh yes, she say, it runs in families – identical twins. Just like Theo and Cleo, I say.

But Mr McClancy say no, they are identikit twins.

Chapter 19

Ola!

I have not been writing to you for a few days because it have been St Patrick Day which, mama y papa, last for a week!

It is the big festival in Ireland because he is their patron saint. Conchubhair tell us all about him in the class. He say that St Patrick bring the shamrock to Ireland and drive out all the snakes, but today they get on Government airplanes and go all over the world. He say they have the right idea because the weather here is always very bad in March.

But I think he is talking about the Government again. He talk about them a lot of the time, and I am being seeing on the television that El Bruton is going to the Casa Blanca in Washington to meet President Clinton. They are having a special concert in honour of the great Irish patriot Jerry Lewis, who have been invited for the first time.

Mrs McClancy say that is not really his name, but Mr McClancy say no it should be Charlie Chaplin because he used to be silent movie star. But now, he say, they can not shut him up. Every time he switch on the television, he see the same mug. I look closely but can only see a face.

I am wondering what will be in the concert, and Mr McClancy say the high light will be El Bruton's imitation of a burro laughing. He hope it not damage the peace process, he say. It should really be Alberto, or even El Bert, say Mr McClancy, but Mrs McClancy say they are all like headless chickens. Maybe the burro noises are a better act, I think, but I do not say.

In the class, Conchubhair is saying that St Patrick bring the faith to Ireland and the Irish bring the faith and begorrah to America. I ask Conchubhair how the Government choose who is to fly all over the world and he say they have a secret lottery. The loser is having to stay and review the parade in Dublin. Conchubhair say this person have to have a cast-iron constitution. Like Dev.

I feel sorry for that person, mama y papa. It is officially the springtime here, but it is like the winter in the Sierra Nevada. It is snowing with the thunder and the hailstones. I think some of the children in the parade have been painting their faces and their knees blue, but no, that is what they are turning.

But there are many visitors, especially from America, where the Irish people all go and become bands. Then their children and grandchildren come back here and play in the St Patrick Day Parade. They are much bigger than the Irish girls, and they do not look cold. Some of them do not play music at all, but just jump around and wave ribbons. That is what Colleen do.

I forget I do not tell you about Colleen. I meet her in the pub after the parade with her friends. She ask me what is the drink I am drinking and I tell her it is Ballysomething. But I get it wrong again, it is really the Baileys. She have one too because it look like a health drink. Her name is Colleen Bucholski from New York, but she say she is Irish. I say I never hear that name before here, but she say it is from Poland like the Pope. But her father marry her mother, who have an Irish granny.

I ask where is the granny, and she say she is in Ohio. But she always tell her about Ireland and Colleen always want to come here, but have been afraid because of the fighting. I ask her what fighting and she look at me very surprised. She ask how I not know about the Irish freedom fighting which have been going on until last year. She say she does not know it is so bad until she is

coming in from the airport in the bus and see all the destruction.

I think she is wrong, but she say oh no, her mother have been telling her all about it and she have been seeing it on the television herself. She say of course I would not know about this because I am from Spain.

Then she start to talk to her friends about a band they hear in New York who sing Irish rap protest songs. They have a singer called Dick O'Lashnikoff who is very funky, say Colleen. He have an Irish girlfriend in the band, but she go out with him once anyway and he is very, very funky.

I ask her what that word mean, but she just laugh and say are we all having another drink? She always want to see a real Irish pub, she say, but this will have to do. I tell her my teacher tell me American girls who come here on St Patrick Day are not allowed out of their hotels in case they meet the natives. But Colleen laugh again and say she know I am not a native. Then she say hey this drink is hot stuff, Pancho, and she wink at her friends. They all start to cough and look at their watches and say they go soon, because they promise to meet the Marines at the hotel. Colleen say maybe she want some Spanish lessons and they laugh.

But why am I in the pub again, mama y papa? It is only because the weather is so bad or I would not go to such a place. It is again very crowded, so that Colleen is having to stand very close to me. She have a very big mouth with many teeth. She ask me to tell her about Madrid and so I am telling her about our apartment in the city and our house in the country, and grandmother's rancho and many other things. Then I tell her about the McClancys and she say they sound like the Adams family, but I do not know them. She laugh again when I say that. She really have many shiny teeth.

I do not remember what happen next, but we are dancing together in a dark place with very loud music and flashing lights. I have tried again to find the place called Lillie's, but a man there say go away they are full, even though I say I am friend of Bono and Van the Man.

I also try to go into a place called El Pod, but two men tell me to go away. They say Colleen can come in if she like but she say no, she is with my Spanish friend. I can not see any Spanish friend, but we get back into taxi and he bring us to this place where we are dancing. It is very crowded and Colleen is having to dance very close to me, even when the music is fast.

I think she is falling asleep and I am holding her up when I hear the loud noises and much shouting at the door. Someone is fighting to get in, and I think I hear some glass breaking. Then a man is shouting, there he is over there, and another man is shouting, let us get the rat. They have very short hair.

Then they come over and one of them start shaking me and the other one grab Colleen. I tell him to let her go but he grab my arm like a pincers. I think the blood is stopping in my veins he is pinching me so hard. He push his face very close to mine and the music is very loud but I think he say, don't truck with the US Marines buddy. I say, oh hello buddy. Then I think I fall on the floor.

When I get up and go back to our table Colleen is gone. But there is a man standing there with a bill. It is for two bottles of wine, but he have the price wrong. I tell him the bill say forty-five pounds, and he say that is right. I tell him he mean maybe five pounds, like in Madrid, but he say, listen sonny me boy, this wine come from grapes brought to Ireland by St Patrick himself and that is the right price here.

It is lucky for me, mama y papa, that I have in my pocket the letter you send me last week with the money. He say he accept pesetas and take it all.

When I go out I look for a taxi but they are all full. Only one of them stop at last, but the driver look out and say Haysoos not you again. Then he drive off.

Chapter 20

April

Ola!

More surprises for the McClancys yesterday, mama y papa! Especially Mrs McClancy, I think.

Their daughter arrive home unexpectantly from America. Maybe that is not the right word, because I hear Cleo telling Theo her sister is expecting. She not say what.

Her name is Ashling and she have her boyfriend with her. His name is Dick Washington and I think he is a basketball player, because he is very tall and look like O.J. Simpson.

Everybody is very surprised when the doorbell is ringing and I open it – the door, I mean. There is a girl with speckles standing there, but before she say anything her friend Dick is jumping up the step and saying, hey man, you must be the brother, give me five.

I do not know what he is talking about, but he grab my hand and hit it, so I nearly fall back into the hall of the McClancy house.

The daughter Ashling is saying no, you must be Haysoos. Then Dick start laughing and say hey man, he always want to meet me, he hear so much about me. I ask him where he hear about me in America and he say all the time when he is small and going to the gospel hall with his family they talk about me all the time. Then he say give me five again, but this time I duck.

Mrs McClancy is coming down the stairs in her dressing gown and asking what am I shouting about, then she see Ashling and the basketball player in the hall. She nearly trip over her dressing gown, but catch the banisters just in time. Sacred heart, she say.

The boyfriend Dick is putting out his hand and I am afraid he is going to ask her for five, but this time he just want to shake it. Mrs McClancy is sitting on the stairs and looking at her daughter with her mouth open. It is Mrs McClancy who have her mouth open, not Ashling.

What, she say at last. Then she say who, looking at Dick Washington, and then she say how and why. (I learn to spell them correctly at last, mama y papa!)

Ashling look at her mother and say, did Dad not tell you then? Mrs McClancy say what again. Then Ashling say she is getting married. Mrs McClancy then say who and why, and then she stop. She look at her daughter again, and then she look at her boyfriend again. Then she start to shout for Mr McClancy.

He come running out of his bedroom and stop when he look down the stairs. Then he say Haysoos, but I know now he not mean me.

Mrs McClancy say is that all you can say? But he look at daughter and say, you did not give me much time to break it. Break what? say Mrs McClancy. Ashling is saying things happen very fast in St Patrick week, and she have been nabbed.

Mrs McClancy is saying what you mean, nabbed? Her daughter say she mean the immigration people made a sweep and she have no papers. So she have been sent packing.

But, say her mother, who this? And she look at Dick Washington. Oh, say Ashling, maybe you better sit down. Mrs McClancy say I am sitting down.

Then her daughter tell her Dick is singing and playing in her band, and then she say he is also her boyfriend.

Mrs McClancy then say, and? Ashling say again, and we are getting married. Very soon, she say. Her mother say, oh no she not believe it, but Dick say oh yes, it true all right. He hope the baby will be born in America and be an American citizen.

Mrs McClancy try to stand up then, but Mr McClancy have to catch her. They all go into kitchen.

I bring in the cases off the steps. When I am doing this I look across the road and see Mrs Young looking out from behind her curtains. I wave but she not wave back.

Now I am having to share my room with Dick Washington, mama y papa! It have two beds so it is okay for me, but he have a bed too small for him because I think he need one three metres long.

The daughter Ashling is sharing the bedroom of Cleo. I think she not happy with this, and Cleo is not happy too.

I am not happy also, because Dick is snoring very loud. And he is sleepwalking also. Last night when I at last go to sleep, I wake up suddenly when I hear a noise. It is Dick and he is sleepwalking. He bump his head off the door, and this is the noise that wake me up, or maybe he say something in his sleep.

I am not awake properly at first, mama y papa, but I get up slowly to see where he is going. I will catch him from falling down the stairs, I think. But then I remember it is dangerous to wake up some person who is doing the sleepwalk because maybe they die of the fright.

Then I hear some terrible shoutings. It is Mr McClancy. I go shh, shh, in case he wake up Dick Washington. Then I hear Dick Washington saying hey man, give me five, so I know he is awake. Mr McClancy say he will give him more than five if he catch his black burro sneaking into his room again. Or any other person's room.

That is when Dick Washington explain he is sleepwalking. But Mr McClancy say sleepwalking my burro.

They talk about burros many times in Ireland, mama y papa, but I never see any.

Chapter 21

Ola!

They are having another meeting of Mrs McClancy's committee today. She want to talk about the planning for the fashion show, but first Mrs Young ask how is her daughter. Mrs McClancy say fine, fine, and start to read a letter she get about the clothes, but Mrs Young ask, is she home on holiday?

Mrs McClancy say that yes, she is home on a short break. Mrs Young is asking, then who is the nice tall young man she have with her? Oh, say Mrs McClancy, he is a friend from America. He is a professor, she say.

I nearly drop the tray with the tea and the biscuits when she say this, and Cedric say I am seeming nervous today. He say I look like I not get much sleep and he is right because Dick is snoring every night. And the sleepwalking he also do every night.

Mrs Lemming say she is worried because she hear the nuns want to sell their land so that poor people will have houses. She hear that they are praying that the next meeting of the council will change the zoning so that the building of the small houses will be starting.

Mrs McClancy snort and say she know that what they really want is more money.

Ms Mimble say she is writing to the times and telling the Irish people that they must save this open space for the nation as a hole.

Cedric say wait a minute, he not want the nation looking over his back wall when he is out in the garden sunning himself.

Not a pretty sight, say Mrs Young, but Cedric say at least he have no problem with sell you light.

Mrs Lemming is saying that she hear there is going to be a big pub and a shopping centre and a fitness centre if the nuns have their way. She hear there are some Mystery Men behind it all, and one of them have a laundry operation.

I am nearly dropping the tray again when I hear this, because I remember that Mercedes family on the Northside have a laundry.

But someone else say no it is the electricity company that is called the BES here, mama y papa. Maybe that what Cedric mean when he say sell you light.

I am going to tell them about Mercedes and the laundry people, but just then there is a terrible noise from upstairs. At first I think it is Theo and Cleo landing an airplane on the house, but no, it is loud, loud music coming from my room. It is someone playing a guitar and jumping on the floor and shouting.

Everybody look frightened when they hear this noise. Mrs McClancy's hand start to shake so that I think she will drop her cup, but she put it down on the table. Haysoos, she say. Yes, I say, but she not mean me. She mean Dick.

Mrs Young ask, is that the professor now? But nobody hear her in the loud noises. He is shouting in a loud voice and saying, hay you mothers, now listen to me I come to tell you bout the trinity, you see this weed, three leaves one stem, that how Patrick is telling dem.

Mrs McClancy ask me to go up and tell them to stop. I go up the stairs and tell them. At first Dick and Ashling are not hearing me, but at last they turn down the amplifier so I can talk to them. Dick is saying, hey Haysoos, you still my main man? I must go down and say how sorry I am. Ashling say no, it is okay, but he follow me anyway.

73

When he walk into the sitting-room everybody nearly drop their cups of tea. Mrs McClancy is trying to speak, and I think at first she have caught a fig roll in her throat, but at last she say this is Mr Washington.

He bow and say how do you do, and Ms Mimble nearly fall off the couch when he bend down to her. But then Cedric stand up and hold out his hand and say, give me five man. And he is hitting Dick's hand. Dick is saying hey man you one of the brothers?

Mrs Young say she not so sure about that, Professor. Dick is saying, hey man who you call a professor? Mrs Young say, who you calling man? And they laugh. Mrs McClancy then say Mr Washington have to leave now because he have an important engagement. But Dick is saying now I told you we not bothered about any engagement, we want to get hitched as quick as possible.

Mrs McClancy is saying very loud to everybody that Mr Washington mean he is going to travel around Ireland using his thumb. That a funny way to travel, I think, but Cedric is saying he can hop into his Cinquecento any time, brother.

Dick is eating the last of the biscuits and saying to Mrs McClancy, hey man what you talking about? I mean we want to get hitched so Ash can come back as Mrs Washington and the baby be born in the USA like Bruce Springsteen. Maybe we even call him Bruce, he say. Or Brucina if it's a girl.

Everybody start talking very loud then and they do not see for a minute that Ashling have come into the room. Then they stop talking again. She look at them and they look at her. Then she go over to Dick and hold his hand and say, this my fiancé Dick Washington, he is a famous singer from America but he have a different name there, he call himself Dick O'Lashnikoff.

I try to remember where I heard that name and then I remember Colleen who tell me about him. Then I remember the Marines and I feel my arm still sore.

Ashling and Dick say goodbye then and go out of the room. Mrs McClancy is trying to pour some more tea into her cup, but is putting it in the saucer instead. Mrs Young is saying what a nice young man you have there, he will make a grand son-in-law. Mrs McClancy smile and say oh yes, they all very excited when they hear the news.

Cedric is saying to Ms Mimble very quietly that it is the baby he feel sorry for. She say what the problem, she know lots of mixed couples these days, but Cedric say no, he mean he feel sorry for the baby because it will have an Uncle Theo and Aunty Cleo.

Mrs McClancy is tapping her spoon on her cup and saying can we get on with the meeting now. Everybody say oh yes, of course of course. Mrs Lemming is talking again about the BES and saying we will have to find out who is behind it.

They ask Mrs McClancy if her husband know anything about it, but Mrs McClancy say he not have anything to do with any kind of laundry.

Mrs Young say no, he not like to wash dirty linen in public.

Cedric say he have a friend in the newspapers and he ask him, but all he hear is roomers, and it all very shady. There is a Mr Big on the Southside, his friend say, pulling all the strings. Cedric say he always want to meet someone with that name.

Chapter 22

Ola!

I have being to an Irish wedding, mama y papa. You remember I tell you about Mrs McClancy's sister Birdie who have a daughter getting married? Well, she get married this week and we all go.

It is the first time I am seeing the outside of Dublin, mama y papa, and it is not like Spain at all at all. It is very wet everywhere when we drive up across Ireland in Mr McClancy's car. When we go through one town, he say this is Alberto's stomping ground. I look out but I do not see him anywhere.

Mrs McClancy say no he is probably in Barbados or Balubaland. I never hear of this other place. Mr McClancy say, oh he travel for the good of the country and this crowd soon do the same. Look at Dick, he say, still hopping on planes and nobody say boo to Mr Clean.

I still do not know who is this Mr Clean, mama y papa. If he is in the government his name never get in the paper.

When Mr McClancy talk about Dick he is not meaning Ashling's boyfriend – they are not coming to the wedding because they have a gig in the country, I hear them say. A gig is an Irish dance, I think. Mr McClancy mean the Foreign Minister, who is also called the Thawnaiste. I ask Conchubhair what that mean and he say it is old Irish word meaning someone who hang you if you look crooked at them. They have some strange words in this old Irish language, mama y papa, they are stranger even than their English words, which I am learning more and more.

Conchubhair say when I go back to Madrid I will be blinding them all with my astonishing vocabulary. Then he teach us all about the Interwoven Adjective. This mean that when you want to make strong what you are saying, instead of saying I am not going anywhere you say I am not going anybleedinwhere. You can also be using other Interwoven Adjectives, he tell us about them some other day.

Mercedes is asking him then where was he on Tuesdaybleedinight, but he just say he tell her after the class if she wait. She say she wait for two hours on Tuesday and he not show up. He say yes yes, he talk about that later, but she say no thank you, I've had ebleedinough. He smile and say that a perfect example of what he teach us. It is called Dublin knees, he say, but he is looking at the San Sebastian knees of Mercedes.

Then she look at me and say she is not washing her hair on Friday night, what am I doing? I tell her I am not washing my hair too. Conchubhair say it all fascibleed-inating.

When we arrive in the McClancy car at the town where Birdie and her family live, we drive past a big harbour where I think they are having a festival. All the boats in the harbour are having flags with a big red leaf in the middle. Mr McClancy is seeing them as well and saying oh-oh to himself. I ask him if it is because of the wedding maybe, but he say no he does not think so. Theo and Cleo wake up suddenly and say that was a very long drive, are we in Canada? I say, don't be silly, that is across the sea.

Then we come to a big house, bigger than the McClancy house, and we drive in the big gates and up to the top of the hill. I think at first it is a hotel, but then the door open and Birdie come out. She say come in, come in. She say it a pity that Dervogilla's cousin Ashling not make it, but Mrs McClancy explain about the gig.

Then Birdie's husband Jim come out. He shake my hand very hard and I think it nearly break, mama y papa, but it is because he is a fisherman and very strong. He say, so you are the Spaniard in the works, and laugh very loud. Then he say, don't worry son, we'll look after you. I tell him I am not worried about anything, but he just laugh even louder and hit me between my shoulders so that I nearly fall in the door.

Everybody in the house is drinking and singing songs, mama y papa. Jim ask me what I have and I say just a Bally or a Bailysomething, but he say no, no, have a real drink. Then he take out a bottle of Canadian Club and pour it. Throw that back, he say, but I drink it instead. I cough because it is not like the Club Orange or the Club Lemon, but much stronger. Jim pour another one and say a bird never flew on one wing.

I am wondering why he is saying this when his wife Birdie come up and take him away to meet some other people. Then she come back to me and say she hear we have some visitors from America in the McClancy house. I tell her that Ashling come home, and she say yes, but not alone she hear. Then I tell her about Dick and she say I see I see well that is a nice kettle of fish. I look around but there is no kettle in the room.

Some other men come over then and are telling me I am very brave to walk into the lion's den, but I tell them they are mixing me with some other person because I am never going to the Dublin zoo. Then they are asking me about swimming. I tell them I learn to swim in Madrid, in my uncle's swimming pool, and one of them say good, maybe I be able to swim with the sea lions. They are all laughing very loud then.

Mr McClancy is standing in the corner talking to his mobile phone. I am very surprised to see this. Everybody in Ireland have a mobile phone, mama y papa, and they get into their cars and drive around all day talking to everyone else in their cars. But Mr McClancy is using his mobile phone when he is not in his car, that is why I am very surprised.

Mrs McClancy is talking to her sister, who say, oh look I see Mick on the blower again. Mrs McClancy look over at Mr McClancy and say oh yes, that is his latest toy. Birdie say is that who he is phoning? And then she laugh. Mrs McClancy is not laughing. She ask Birdie how is the fishing, because she hear they are catching some strange fish up here these days.

Her sister say oh the fishing is fine, but what is this she hear about Ashling's big catch in New York? Mrs McClancy ask her what she mean, and Birdie say Haysoos have been telling me all about her big boyfriend. Is he tall, dark and handsome, she ask. Mrs McClancy say Derv's husband-to-be is certainly not falling into that category, but Birdie say no, but he is a doctor.

Mrs McClancy is seeing me listening. She come over and say maybe I go and find Theo and Cleo because she not see them for a while. I say goodbye to my new friends and they say *adios*, which is very nice to be hearing after so long from home. I go out then and look for Theo and Cleo.

After much searching I find them in the town, where they are playing with a machine you put money in and win more money. But Theo is crying because he put all his money in and not win. Cleo is also crying. I ask her did you put your money in also, but she say no, Theo did.

Then I say I will get it back. I put some money in the machine and push the buttons. At first nothing happen and then, mama y papa, there is much noise and flashing lights and many many Irish pesetas are coming out of the machine. I am picking up as many of them as I can catch, and so also are Theo and Cleo. Theo is saying it worked, it worked, and is holding up a piece of long flat plastic thing which he wave over his head.

Then I hear a roar and a man come over shouting at us with a big red face. You fix the machine, he shout. No, I say, you fix the machine. What, he roar, it not broken. Then he try to catch my sleeve. But I hear a loud crashing and the machine fall on floor. It broken now, shout Theo and many people come to help the man to pick up the money. I want to stay and help but Theo and Cleo pull me out the door.

When we get back to the house, Mrs McClancy is saying where did you get to, and Theo and Cleo say oh we just look around the town. She say it is time for dinner and I hope you not getting chips in the town, and Theo say no but Haysoos nearly have his.

Chapter 23

¡Ola!

Last night I stop writing because everybody is singing and I have to sing also. I am singing some of the old songs my grandmother teach me. Everybody say they are very nice, but someone want me to sing 'Guantanamera' and someone else ask me do I know there is a valley in Spain called Jarama. I tell him maybe I find it on the map and he look strange.

But now I tell you about the wedding. Next morning we all go to the church for the wedding. There is a man there with a television camera and I think it is going to be on the television news. I tell Theo and Cleo that their uncle must be important man to have wedding on television, but Mr McClancy say he may be a big fish here but that not mean much in Dublin. Then he explain that it is an old Irish tradition to have your wedding on the videotape.

The man with the television camera is walking backwards up the church when Dervogilla is arriving. She look a bit like Ashling only thinner, I think. When the television man is beside our seat I hear Mr McClancy saying something about the local Cecil B The Mill, but Mrs McClancy look cross and say shh, shh, he is very high-priced and come all the way from Dublin. All her friends use him at their weddings, she say. Mr McClancy say, well we won't, that's for sure. Then the television man nearly bump into the priest who is standing at the altar. The priest say sorry, sorry and get out of his way.

The wedding take a long time, mama y papa, because the television man make them do everything two times. Then we go outside and get into cars, but the television man say everybody get out of the cars for more pictures. Mr McClancy is saying he not a Hollywood extra, but the man say oh no, he have heard of him and know he is an important man in Dublin. He must think Mr McClancy is a dancer, mama y papa, because he say he hear he is a mover and a shaker.

Mr McClancy laugh and say where did he hear that, and the television man say he hear it from a wild woman. He then ask did the video do the trick with the councillor? Mr McClancy then say in a very quiet voice, okay, okay, where do you want me to stand?

There is more television and more pictures when we get to the hotel. Birdie's husband own half the hotel. There is also a lady taking pictures for the town paper. Birdie's husband Jim own half of that, too. The woman ask me am I a relation of the bride or groom, and I say no, I am from Spain. She say oh really, and take my picture anyway.

Then she go and take pictures of some politicians who are there. Some of them are friends of Birdie's husband Jim, and Mr McClancy say the other politicians are there because they might be his friends next year. Jim like to play both sides against the middle, he say. I think he is talking about another old Irish sport, mama y papa.

There are many speeches at the dinner, which go on for a long time. Even one of the politicians is standing up to make a speech. Someone near me is saying he is greener than the greens, but he have orange hair. He is saying he know Derv and Tom all their lives and he is very pleased to see they are going to help the African people just like their forefathers in the missions did for many centuries. The priest is laughing when he say this, the just look puzzled and mop his orange hair. It move and down.

Then we go into the ballroom for the dancing. There is a terrible band there, mama y papa. They are playing very strange music, and there is a singer who look like one of the plastic men in the shop windows of Madrid. He have the same staring eyes and the shining suit and the hair that look like the wind never blow it.

I hear Jim saying to Mr McClancy that they could not get the group called Wee Dan Niell but this fellow is the next best thing.

There are many beautiful Irish girls at the wedding, mama y papa, but some of them have such strange accents that I think at first they are from some other country. The band is telling everyone to get up and dance, so I go and ask one of the bridesmaids to dance with me. She is talking to one of the men who have been asking me about lions and swimming the night before, but she dance with me anyway and he look annoyed.

She tell me her name is Majella and I tell her my name, but she is not laughing. I ask her if she live here and she say no, she is here on holidays. Her friend who is dancing near us hear her say that and say it is not a holiday, she is on leave from active service. Then I think she is a nurse, but she laugh and say no, but she have seen a lot of people stitched up. She ask me how long am I staying in the free state. I do not know what she mean by that, but she say that is where you are now. I say I have not been seeing much things free in the shops, and she laugh again and say I am funny person.

Majella is asking me about where I live in Spain and is saying I must be a very rich person, but I say no, of course not, we only have an apartment in Madrid and one house in the country, which is much smaller than grand-mother's rancho. She say that still sound very nice to her. The music stop but she keep holding my hand and say she like some fresh air. We go out onto the balcony and talk, but I see her friend following us. I ask Majella is he a fisherman, but she laugh and say no, but he have caught some big fish off guard where she come from.

When we come in to dance again, her friend is inside the door, and he is talking to some more of his friends. The band is playing 'Viva Espana' – you know that song, mama y papa, it is the one the British tourists always sing when they are getting off the airplanes in Spain and falling down the steps. The band is playing it now and everyone start doing funny dances, I think they are thinking they are doing Spanish dances, but they look like the wild bulls all crashing and bumping together, with much steam coming off their backs. The men look like this also.

Majella is grabbing me by the hand and saying come on Haysoos, you show them a proper Spanish dance. At first I do not want to, but she squeeze my hand and look in my eyes so that I forget everything else, but I remember the many lessons I have been getting as a boy at the academy of Doña Maria Elena Cantril. I jump into the middle of the floor and stomp my feet. Everybody else stop dancing, then the band start playing the Paso Doble, mama y papa, and my feet are hitting the floor so fast I think maybe my teeth fall out!

Majella is clapping and dancing beside me, and someone have giving her a carnation which she is holding between her teeth. The music is getting faster and louder, and I am whirling Majella around and around. She is giving me the carnation from her mouth into my mouth. Everybody is clapping and laughing, and the room is going around faster and faster.

Suddenly I am crashing into the crowd and my elbow is hitting the mouth of Majella's friend. He fall but get up again and hit me in the nose. Majella is shouting stop, stop, but he is saying, who does he think he is Michael Fuckinflatley, well I'll flatten him.

He try to punch my nose again, but I duck and he hit someone else instead. This man shout hey and try to hit him back, and a lot of people suddenly are starting to hit other people's noses. I am crawling under a table to get out of the way, but then I hear the band making a very loud noise with the drums, and the singer is saying ladies and gentlemen as a special surprise for you all the way from Noo York City, we present Dick O'Lashnikoff!

The curtains go back then, and it is Dick and Ash and some other musicians! Everybody is clapping, except Mrs McClancy, who is looking at her sister, who is looking first at Mrs McClancy and then at Ash and then at Mrs McClancy again. She say something to her and smile and count on her fingers, but Mrs McClancy still not smile. Everybody else is still clapping.

The band start playing some very loud music, and Dick is jumping around the stage and shouting, Listen everybody 'cause I'm talkin' to you, we all got to play a part and see this thing through, there is only one way to end this mess, we gotta take part in de peace process.

But just then he see me under the table and shout hey, Haysoos, give me five. I stand up then, but Majella's friend shout, oh there he is the wee Spanishite, and he throw a chair at me.

That when the trouble start, mama y papa. When Dick see the chair miss my head but not the window, he shout hey, who throw a chair at my main man Haysoos? Then he jump off the stage onto the back of Majella's friend, who spin around like a toreador with the cape on his shoulders, but Dick is biting him on the neck so he not fall off easily. The man is screaming very loud which mean that his friends come to help him. But Dick is jumping around and doing the karate kicks. I am helping a little bit with the fork I find under the table, and the other musicians are also joining in.

Everybody is hitting everybody else, except the bride and groom who have been up in their room getting ready to go away on the honeymoon. When they come down the stairs, they see everybody on the whole floor of the ballroom hitting and shouting and biting and spitting. Dervogilla is stopping on the stairs and screaming stop,

stop everybody, but nobody can hear her because they all make too much noise themselves.

But suddenly there is a much louder noise that frighten everybody.

It is a gun.

Crack, crack, crack it go very loud. Majella and her friends dive under the tables, and some of them are hitting their pockets with their hands. Everybody else stop fighting and turn around with their hands up. I am doing this too.

Then we look up onto the balcony that run around the ballroom and see Theo and Cleo. Theo have a gun in his hand and he wave it around. It go crack again. The bullet hit the ceiling and everybody hit the floor.

Mr McClancy shout up at last, where the hell did you get that? Theo and Cleo point up at the ceiling and say in the attic, there is loads more there.

(He mean are not is, mama y papa, I am learning all the time.)

Chapter 24

Ola!

Well, I am safe back in Dublin, mama y papa! I do not think I want to go to the country again. What happen after Theo is shooting the gun? Well, of course the police are coming very quickly with their cars making loud noises with their sirens. There are many of them and I think I see soldiers as well in a big lorry.

At the same time when they are coming I look out the window at the back of the hotel and see the man with the orange hair climbing out of the toilet window. It is not even the caballero's toilet, mama y papa, so maybe he go in there by mistake and have to come out again in a hurry. He must be very ashamed of this mistake, mama y papa, because he run away across the fields. While he is running he hold onto his hair.

There are many pictures of the wedding in the papers, even here in Dublin. I am saying at the breakfast table that I did not know Birdie's husband Jim was such important a man, and Mr McClancy is saying, well he certainly is now.

I learn new English words from the papers. 'Cache' is one of them. I ask if this mean the same as cash, and Mr McClancy say that where Jim is concerned he would not be at all surprised.

I am sending you the papers so you can see them for yourself. They have pictures of Jim and Birdie and Dervogilla and her new husband. And they have pictures also of Majella and her friends getting into a big van.

Some of them have black eyes and bandages on their heads. 'Police brutality alleged' is another phrase I learn from the paper.

There is also a picture of Theo and it say BOY HERO OF MASSIVE ARMS HAUL.

The paper is also saying that police suspect the arms may have been brought in by a foreign trawler, and it say they are seeking a mysterious Spanish-looking visitor who may be able to help them in their inquiries. I wonder who it can be, mama y papa, because I see nobody like that when I am there.

Mrs McClancy is looking at the paper too and looking very happy. She is saying she never enjoy a wedding so much in years. I think this is a strange thing to say, mama y papa, because her sister and her sister's husband have being arrested by the police after they find all the guns in the fish-boxes in the attic of the hotel. And Dervogilla's husband is saying he want a divorce.

But there is no divorce in Ireland, mama y papa, so Mrs McClancy is saying he is stuck with her now. Mr McClancy say maybe he should stay in Ireland instead of going to the Third World, because there are enough balubas here to sort out. Mrs McClancy say that is not a nice thing to say about them. He say who do you mean, the balubas or your relations?

Theo and Cleo come down the stairs then and start fighting because Cleo is not having her picture in the paper. She is saying she find the guns, not Theo, but he is telling the police and the lady from the paper that it was him. Mrs McClancy say you mean it was he, but Cleo say no it was her. Mrs McClancy say how you expect Haysoos to learn any English when you do not speak it properly?

Cleo say she not care about speaking it properly, she just want her picture in the paper too so all her friends at school see it. Theo is pointing his finger at her and shouting bang, bang.

Just then there is a ring ring on the front door and I open it. There is a man from the television station there and he have other men with cameras and lights. The man have a microphone and he is shouting into it, I am now standing outside the home of the boy hero and he have just opened the door, no wait a minute, shag it this not him, sorry, is this where the McClancys live?

Mrs McClancy is coming to the door then and pushing me out of the way. She say, hello Charlie, I'm glad you got my little letter about the open space but I did not expect you to turn up so quick and catch me in my dressing gown. She is saying give me five minutes to get ready, and then she scream, oh my God is that thing switched on? Then she push me out of the way again and run back in the door and up the stairs. I think she not want the camera to see her dressing gown because it say Copthorne Tara Hotel on it.

The man she call Charlie look at me and ask what all this about. I tell him I not know either. The man with the camera is saying he not see anyone move so fast since Sonia break the world record. The man called Charlie is asking me who I am, and I tell him I am the au pair. The man with the camera look at me and say Haysoos, some au pair. Then Charlie is asking where is the boy wonder, but Mrs McClancy is coming down the stairs again dressed in her best clothes.

She come out on the step again and say now, I show you what the residents' committee want. She open a big map and start showing it to Charlie and saying, now we do not mind if people are getting houses, but this not a suitable area. Charlie is trying to talk to her but she keep going very fast, saying some people are saying we just afraid our houses not have the same value but that is a lie.

She say she want the nuns to come out in the open about their plans and she hope the Mother Superior will come out of the bunker. Then she say to Charlie, no maybe you better not use that last bit, it make her sound like Hitler even if she do have a moustache. Then she give a little scream and say, oh my God I hope you can wipe that bit.

Charlie then tell her to relax, the camera is not switched on. She say, oh thank God, I'll start again but I'm very nervous. The camera man is saying it not the only thing not switched on. Charlie is saying wait a minute, wait a minute, I think we have crossed wires here. She say okay, I wait till you fix them, but that is not what he mean at all. He tell her then that he want to meet her son Theo. She say oh, and then say, I think he is gone to school already.

But Theo is coming out just then and waving at the camera. He also wave at Mrs Young who is looking out her window. But she drop the curtain and not wave back. The man called Charlie is asking if it is okay to talk to him and Mr McClancy come out then and say of course it is, but of course his solicitor will be watching the news that night. The man with the camera then start shaking and nearly drop the camera, and say, oh my God now I'm really frightened, but Charlie is asking him to quit the messing.

Then they are asking Theo to say again how he find the guns and what happen then. Theo is telling them a big long story about how he go up an old ladder with broken steps and cobwebs and find a creaky trapdoor that he is pushing up very slowly. I do not understand this because the hotel is being built in 1991 and have a stairs which go into the attic with not a trapdoor, just a door with no traps.

He is also not mentioning Cleo at all, but just then she open a window upstairs and shout down at them that Theo is a lying little git. She is shouting that she is the person who really find the guns and she can prove it. They are all looking up at her, and then Charlie say the thing you hear in all the American TV stories, mama y papa – he shout, oh my God she have a gun.

I look up and Cleo is waving a big black gun out the window. Mrs McClancy scream and dive into the flower bed.

Everybody else is shouting and jumping as well, and then she pull the trigger. I close my eyes because and feel wet stuff hitting my face. Blood, I think. Is this the end of Haysoos?

Then I open my eyes and, mama y papa, I am still alive! I forget she is having a water pistol.

Charlie look at the cameraman and the man with the lights. They are looking at Charlie and they all shake their heads. They say thank you very much and start to go away, but Mrs McClancy is running after them and saying what about the open space and the recreation centre. The cameraman is saying what you need here missus is a detention centre.

Chapter 25

Ola!

You remember I mention to you that Mercedes tell me she is not washing her hair some night. Well, mama y papa, last night was the night.

She mention it again when I am talking to her in the class and she is saying how she like to spend a whole evening speaking the Spanish instead of the English because it make her very tired sometimes trying to understand what everyone is saying. I say yes, it must be even harder when she live on the Northside, but she say that is just rubbish and not to believe everything Conchubhair say.

I know what she mean because today he have been telling us about the drinking laws here in Ireland, mama y papa, and how they change them. He tell us that the Government is deciding last year to crack down on the drinking drivers. That mean the drivers who go into the pubs and are drinking many drinks and then getting into their cars and trying to drive them home. Sometimes, he say, they get into the back seat and try to drive the car from there.

I do not believe him when he is saying this, but that is not all he say. He tell us then that the Government bring in new laws to make the drivers stop drinking and make the roads safe. I say to him that must make everybody very happy but he laugh, hah, like that, and say you must be joking. He tell us then that the Government come up against the Publican Movement. I say ah yes, Gerry

Adams, but he say hah again and say he only in the half-peseta place.

Conchubhair say that the Publican Movement nearly bring the government down. I am going to say I think it is the Thorny Generals who do that, but he say, listen Franco, forget the Thorny Generals, you not in Madrid now. Mercedes then say to him why is he talking like that, and he say he is trying to give a class here but people keep interrupting. She say oh, and is your wife keeping interrupting as well when you at home?

This surprise me because I do not know Conchubhair is married. He say, wife, what you mean wife? I do not have a wife. But Mercedes say, oh then, who was that woman with the small boy and girl I see you with in Herbert Park on Sunday? He say oh, you mean my sister, what were you doing in Herbert Park? She say she not look like a sister to me and why the children call their uncle daddy?

I am very confused and do not understand what Mercedes is saying, but when I look at Conchubhair's face I know that I am only in the half-peseta place. He laugh and say it is an old Irish custom, but when he see us all write it down he say no forget I say that. Mercedes say she won't. He say he can explain everything later but Mercedes say no thanks, I think I understand the situation.

I think her English is very much better than mine, mama y papa, but that is because she have been having extra private lessons from Conchubhair I think.

He start talking again now about the Publican Movement. He say that when the people of Ireland hear from the government that they can not be drinking and driving any more they get on their high horses. I think this is more dangerous myself, mama y papa, but Conchubhair say that what they do.

The people are saying it wipe out all social life in the villages all over the country, and people are writing in the papers and talking on the radio, saying that the people who live outside the villages have magic cars that know their own way home. Then the Publican Movement march on the government and nearly bring it down, Conchubhair say. So the government is getting cold feet and changing the law. Now, he say, you will not be arrested unless you are knocking down the policeman with the breathalyser.

That is a little bag, mama y papa, for blowing into to find out if you have been drinking too much. If it change colour you are slightly drunk, say Conchubhair, and if the policeman change colour you are really drunk.

I think that is what Mercedes mean when she say she not to believe everything Conchubhair is saying. Then she tell me she want to go to a movie picture for which she is already getting the tickets. I am saying then that I not washing my hair either, so we go to the cinema-house which is a big place with many small cinemas inside it.

We are going to see an old Irish film, mama y papa, which they are showing in one of the cinemas. It is called *El Hombre Pacifico*, and the stars of it are a woman actor called Maureen and a man actor called Wayne.

He is still very popular here in Ireland, mama y papa, because most of the small boys have his name. In the cinema-house I hear the mothers shouting at them, Wayne get your hand out of those sweets, and Wayne I told you we need only one bucket not five. That is because they are having the popcorn here in big buckets, mama y papa, and the Coca-Cola in smaller ones with the lids on. This make the cinemas very noisy sometimes, so I hope we can hear *El Hombre Pacifico*.

But he is not really *pacifico* at all. He is shouting and punching another big man and they fall into the river but keep on fighting. Mercedes is laughing and holding my hand all the time, and when he grab Maureen off the train and drag her across the fields I think she is going to choke on her popcorn she laugh so much. I start to hit her on her

94

back, but a man behind me shout hey leave her alone. I turn around and start to explain that it is the popcorn, but then other people are saying, shh shh, we are trying to hear the effinbleedinfilm.

I try to tell them too, but now Mercedes is really choking, I think. I jump up and shout help help, but everybody shout, sit down, you gobshite. I turn around to say something else, but now everybody is shouting. Mercedes is suddenly getting out of her seat and running up the aisle. I think she is really sick so I run after her, but outside the door she is not sick at all but laughing and laughing. I tell her I not think the picture so funny, but she say it was not the picture. I say but we miss the end, and she say it not matter because she will buy the video. The family she stay with can get them very cheap, she say.

We are walking to the house where she stay then, and she say maybe I like a cup of tea or coffee before I get my two buses home to the McClancy house. Inside her Irish house is different from mine. It is smaller but have much more furniture in it. It also have many television sets and many video-recorders. It must be a very big family, I say to Mercedes, but she say sometimes there are many people there and sometimes not so many, she is not sure if they are all in the same family.

I wish to go to the toilet but when I go upstairs I first go into wrong room. It is an office, I think, because there are some of the family in there counting the money from the laundry. When I look in the door and say sorry, they are saying Haysoos to each other, so I think Mercedes have been telling them I am coming for the cup of coffee. Then they start to tidy up the money very quickly and I ask them where is the caballeros, I mean the toilet please.

When I go down the stairs again to the kitchen, one of the men is coming down a few minutes after me. I think he is the father of the house because he say hello Merc to Mercedes. He ask me how long I am here, and I say since before Christmas, but he say no, he mean how long am I up the stairs looking into the office room. When I tell him I just look in the door he say good, good, and pour himself a cup of coffee. Then I ask him how is the laundry business going and he nearly drop it.

He ask me what I mean, and I tell him Mercedes tell the class about how her Irish family have a laundry. Mercedes nod her head and say yes, that she hear them talking about it. The father listen to her and say oh yes, that is right of course, but then he tell us not to say it again to anybody because they are having some trouble with the taxman. He say, but maybe the taxman lose his shirt.

Then he say that remind him. He look at me and say, so you are staying with the McClancy family, and how is Mick treating you? I ask him how he know that, but he laugh and say Dublin is a very small town. Just watch your step, he say then, and go back upstairs.

After that, I talk Spanish with Mercedes until it is time to go home to the McClancys. It is so nice that it remind me of home – but I know that soon in a few months many of my Spanish friends will be here to talk Spanish with me. I am looking forward so much to meeting them all: Adolfo, Alfonso, Antonio, Antonia, Battista, Carlos, Cristos, Conchita, Carmen, Isabella, Isidor, Jose Maria, Javier, Luisa, Luis, Maria, Miguel, Pablo, Pedro, Pilar, Rodriguez, and all the others. It will be like having Madrid here in Dublin, mama y papa!

Chapter 26

Late April

Ola!

Two more exciting things have been happening here at the McClancy home, mama y papa! The big fashion show have been happening for Mrs McClancy – and Dick and Ashling are having become famous!

Also there have been some changes in the committee, but I begin at the starting.

First I forget to tell you about how Dick and Ashling have come home from the wedding of Dervogilla and the doctor. After the helicopter land with them on the nuns' ground they explain to the McClancys that first Dick have been arrested by the policemen because he is throwing two of Majella's friends out of the hotel window. It is on the ground floor, but they land on the car of the politician with the red head who have remembered to come back for it. He is driving the car when Majella's friends land on the roof, so he nearly crash it.

Dick tell us the policemen bring him to the station, and Ashling go along, too. At first the sergeant in the station think he is a Spanish sailor, mama y papa! He is telling them that no, he is a citizen of the United States of America and he plead the fifth. They say that not work here in Ireland, and he say okay then he plead the first, second and third instead. The sergeant say he sound like Groucho Marx, but Dick say no, he more like Harpo because he say nothing, man.

Ashling is telling them that he is a poet, but the sergeant start laughing. But then another policeman come in and say hey, you are Dick Washington alias O'Lashnikoff. Dick ask him how he know that and he say he have been on holiday with his cousin in New York and they hear his band in the Irish pubs. Then he ask him to sign his name in a book. Dick say oh no, man, he not sign his name in any book, he have seen too many of the brothers get shafted with confessions this way.

The sergeant say oh, are you a brothers boy, but Dick say who you calling boy, man? Ashling explain that the sergeant not mean it like that, that he think he go to school with the Christian Brothers. Dick say oh yes, of course he do, all the brothers were Christian in his school.

But the other policeman is saying it not that kind of book, he want Dick's autograph because he never meet a star before. The sergeant say what are you talking about, and Dick and Ashling ask him that too. The policeman just look at him, they tell us later, with his mouth wide open just like President Clinton. Then he say, do you mean to tell me you do not know you are in the charts?

The sergeant say again what are you talking about, but Dick and Ashling are shouting, you mean our record has taken off? And the policeman is saying it not only take off, it have gone into orbit. But nobody know where you are, he tell them, and all the TV and radio and paper people are looking for you.

It is a record they make before they come home, mama y papa, but they are not thinking it will be a big hit. But now everyone in New York and also from the rest of America is wanting to know who is Dick O'Lashnikoff and who is the girl who sing with him on the record. Ashling tell us it is called 'Processed Peace' and it is a rap song.

Conchubhair is saying that rap mean it not have any real tune, just a lot of words nobody can hear, but everyone always think they mean something bad. He say

the rap singers sometimes do their songs standing on their heads and he think that is how they write them sometimes too.

But I am telling you about Dick and Ashling coming home in the helicopter. That happen when Dick ask the sergeant can he make a phone call and the sergeant say okay. Dick is phoning the record company in America and asking them if it is true about the record, and when they hear who it is they are getting very excited and make many phone calls. That is how it only half an hour later when the helicopter come to bring them to Dublin.

The record company want Dick and Ashling to fly back to America, but Dick say wait a minute, we have to get married first because she have no visa. The record company say okay, get it done quick in a registry office, but Mr and Mrs McClancy say no way, it have to be a proper Catholic marriage in a church. This is the first time, mama y papa, that I am really sure they are Catholic.

So Dick and Ashling stay here and the record company go mad. But then they say they arrange for many TV and radio and paper people to fly over and talk to them here.

When Mrs McClancy here this I think she is going to burst. But Mr McClancy say this mean we have no private life left at all. Then Mrs McClancy say why, what guilty secret have he got to keep from the world's press? They not interested, she say, in his fancy woman.

Mr McClancy say he have no fancy woman, but she say she hear him on the phone telling some woman he like her lap top.

Mr McClancy put down his cup and say that is a computer, for heaven's sake, and the woman is a business contact. Mrs McClancy say oh yes, she know the kind of contact he mean. Then she ask Dick and Ashling would they like to play the music for her fashion show.

Ashling is saying, oh this very sudden. She tell her mother she have being thinking her mother not want anyone to know she marrying a rap singer from New York. Now she not sure if it possible to fit in the fashion show, they so busy.

But Dick say give me five Mrs McClancy, it is cool. She give him five. Then he ask can he call her mother? She say I suppose so. Mr McClancy then say he hope Dick not want to call him one two. I am still not understanding everything they say here, mama y papa.

The night the fashion show happen I go with Mercedes. It is in very big hotel which have a pool in the ballroom. At first I think the models are all walking up and down on the water, mama y papa, but then I see it is a very low bridge made of glass or maybe it is strong plastic. Mercedes say she hope no fat models come out or maybe it will break, but I say no they all very thin. She ask me how I know that and I tell her I meet them earlier when they practise, because I am helping Mrs McClancy with the clothes.

I think Mercedes look a bit cross when I say that, but then there is some very loud music and Dick's band start to play. There are many people there from the TV and the radio and papers, and they all start to take pictures then. Some of them are pushing other people to get closer to the band. A wild-looking woman keep standing in front of the band and smiling and waving at the cameras. Mercedes is asking who is that baluba, and then I see it is not a wild woman, it is Mrs McClancy who have changed her hair. It look like an accident. She look taller and she have changed her dress. It have no back and not much front. Also I think she is wearing the things underneath they are calling the ola muchachos.

She keep smiling at the cameras, but the camera people are pushing her out of the way. Then I see she go to talk to some of the women from the papers who have their notebooks with them. They are looking at the models and the band, but Mrs McClancy keep talking to them anyway in a loud voice. I hear her telling them that her future son-in-law is delighted to help in such a good cause. They ask her what cause is that, and she is saying it about preserving the green belt. I not see any models wearing a green belt.

She is telling them then about the nuns and the committee, but someone ask her how her daughter meet her future husband. Mrs McClancy say that she study in the same college in New York, but first she study here and get two degrees. One woman say to the other women and then she meet the son of the three degrees. The other women all laugh at this and write it down, but Mrs McClancy not understand the joke, like me, mama y papa.

When the show is coming to the end, all the models are walking out together in their bathing suits and waving to the crowd. The camera people and the television people are taking many pictures. Then everybody shout for Dick, so he have to come out with Ashling and they have their pictures taken also with the models. He put his arm around one of them and Ashling laugh and pretend she going to push him in the pool. The cameras flash more and more and everybody laugh.

Some of the other committee people are coming out and bowing then, especially Cedric, who have a white suit. Mrs McClancy say excuse me to the women, and she jump up to stand in front with Dick and Ashling. But when she get to the middle of the bridge there is a very loud crack, mama y papa. Mrs McClancy start to wobble and waving her arms. She nearly fall off the bridge, but Dick grab her and pull her back. Her dress start to tear then and she start to fall back again.

This time everybody try to grab her, but she bring them all down with her.

It is like a thundering storm, mama y papa, because the bridge make such a noise when it break, and the flashing from the cameras is like the lightning, only much brighter. I hear Cedric shouting, someone throw me a boy. The pool get very full of bodies, and the water is flooding out all over the place, like the Guadalquivir when the snow melt on the high sierras.

I run to help, and I am glad because I save one of the models from drowning. She is nearly losing her bathing suit, but I get her out and give her the mouth-to-mouth regurgitation, which take a long time. This model not know very much about the regurgitation because she is suddenly opening her eyes and slapping my face. I go then to look for Mercedes, but she have gone home already.

There are many pictures of the fashion show in the papers and on the television, but Mrs McClancy is not being happy at all, mama y papa. Mr McClancy is looking at the papers and saying it look like the *Titanic*. Then he ask who is that strange-looking biddy floating around in front like a melted iceberg? This is the first time I see a grown-up Irish woman crying, mama y papa.

I do not know yet what a biddy is, but I also learn another new English word which is in all the papers. It nearly sound Spanish. It is 'fiasco'.

Chapter 27

Ola!

I forget to tell you, mama y papa, about the losing of the committee members I mention in my last letter! But so many things are happening here at the same time that I forget my own hat next!

There have been another meeting of Mrs McClancy's committee, but some of them are not in the room when I bring in the tea and the fergle cakes. I am hoping they are not drowned in the pool.

Mrs Young is saying, well no publicity is bad publicity, but Mrs McClancy is saying she is consulting her legal advisers about the things the paper is saying about her. Cedric say, oh look at the funny side like him.

Mrs McClancy say what funny side? She not ever be able to darken the door of Patrick Gilbow again. And she run a mile if she ever bump into Norma or Margaret. Mrs Young say that make a change from running after them. Then she say look on the bright side – it just as well Gay and Kay never show up at the fashion show. Mrs McClancy ask what so good about that, and Mrs Young say because maybe he drown and Mrs McClancy be blamed for putting the whole country into the morning.

Cedric laugh and say bar one. Mrs Young ask what one, and he say Mr Duffy who is the air a parent.

Mrs McClancy say what really upset her is what the Sunday paper say about the show. I am seeing the paper and not understanding why she is being upset. It show her picture, not the one where she nearly drown, but one they take earlier before the dress get wet, and I think the picture-man is standing on a chair. The words say 'suburban housewife takes big plunge', and it also say she get in over her head.

The paper also mention Mr McClancy who is not even being there that night, and it say he well known for pushing the boat out and being in hot water too. It hope they not both end up floating alone, or should it be a loan, like he do before, when he nearly go under at Cheltenham but get bailed out by offshore merchantmen.

I ask Conchubhair in the class what all these words mean, but he say you have to read between the lines. I screw up my eyes very small and look and look, mama y papa, but there is nothing between the lines. Sometimes I think Conchubhair is mad.

He have been mad since Mercedes ask him if he is married. Some days he just look out the window and say um to himself, and some days he is smoking when nobody is allowed to be smoking. But he say they are special cigarettes, man.

I ask Mercedes when we are going to the cinema again, but she say she is washing her hair every night for the next two weeks. She must have the cleanest hair in all of the Iberian peninsula, mama y papa!

Then she ask me how is my mermaid friend? I ask her what mermaid friend, and she say the one I pull from the pool. I explain again that I save her from drowning, but she say she I have been watching *Baywatch* too many times. I tell her then that the model is hitting me in the face, and she say good.

I am remembering this at the committee meeting when Cedric ask me why I am smiling. I say sorry I did not mean to smile because it is so sad about the fashion show, but Mrs Young say not really, we made lots of money.

Mrs McClancy look at her watch then and wonder where is Ms Mimble and Mrs Lemming, who is the treasurer. She will give us a full report, she say, but she have not been getting Barbara on the phone for two days.

Cedric say that is strange because he sometimes play bridge with Ms Mimble on Sunday nights, and she not at the last game though she never miss a bridge game. Mrs Young say he should not mention bridges in front of Mrs McClancy.

I look out the window and see the postman going away from the front door, so I go and bring in the postcard. It have a nice picture of Malaysia. Mrs McClancy say she not know anyone in Malaysia but she ask me to read it out loud to practise my English.

The card say, *Sorry everybody but we knew no other way. We realise it be a shock but we seize this big chance to get away. We can no longer keep secret our special. Love, Barbara and Mims.*

When I finish, nobody say anything for a long time. I am thinking maybe I read it out wrong. But Cedric just shake his head and keep saying well, well, well, well, well.

But Mrs McClancy not look well.

Chapter 28

May

Ola again, mama y papa!

Everybody in Ireland go mad this month. Of course I have been telling you they are all mad already, especially the McClancy family who I stay with, but this month the whole country go much madder than ever, mama y papa! The McClancys also. It is because of the Eurovision Song Contest.

Ireland keep winning it and then everybody say they don't want to win it again, but when they do the whole country go mad again and are dancing in the pubs. I am wishing sometimes we could have such excitements in Madrid, but it is so long since Spain have won that it was before I was born. I remember how you used to tell me the story, mama y papa, when I was a very small Spanish boy, about how Spain won the Eurovision in 1968.

How proud I used to feel, mama y papa, when you told me again and again about the night in London, the capital of Royaume Uni, when their great champion, El Cliff, thought he was beating the whole world by singing 'Congratulations', but then at the last minute he was beaten by our own lovely Massiel, singing that beautiful song, 'La La La La'.

Many of the words of it are still in my head, mama y papa, because our English au pair used to sing them to me all the time in my cot. (Why did she sing in my cot, mama y papa, when I had to sleep on the floor? I think she was a very strange person.)

I am writing this before the Contest is being shown.

I will be thinking of you watching it in Madrid, and of my grandmother on her rancho in the Finca de Naranjuez who throw pigeon's eggs at the screen when the other countries are winning. But I am hoping we will win when Anabel Conde sing for us 'Vuelve Conmigo' by José Maria Puron. Everybody here of course think Ireland win it again, especially the interval.

That is all they talk about here, mama y papa, because last year they are having the Riverdance which I mention earlier. Of course I tell everybody it is really the Spanish dancing which they are stealing, but they do not listen. Then they make the interval into a whole show, which tour the world. Of course they can not do this without a real Spanish dancer, Maria Pages, but I do not say this out loud.

Mercedes is liking the American Senor Flatley who dance like a matador who have the cicadas in his pants, but I like it when all the Irish girls in the little black dresses come out and rattle their shoes. The night we go to that show with the whole class, they are having to stop me getting onto the stage to show them my *paso doble*. When the dancing is starting, I am getting out of my seat very quickly, but the ushers catch me when I am climbing onto the stage.

I try to tell them it is an old Spanish tradition but when they tell me about some old Irish traditions I decide to sit down again.

Well, mama y papa! I am writing this later and of course we did not win again, but it have been exciting. And it even more exciting watching it in the McClancy house, because the camera show the audience all clapping and cheering at the end. Ireland say they win anyway because Norway use an Irish violinist and an Irish tune. But there in the middle of all the cheering people we are seeing Mr McClancy. And Ms Wilde.

I think I am imagining it when I see them, but I know I am not by the way Mrs McClancy spill her gin and tonic. Cedric from the committee is watching it with us and he say well, well, well at the same time. And Theo and Cleo say, hey, there's that woman who was here one day. Mrs McClancy ask what day, but they say it a long time ago. They think she is a film star because she drive a sports car, but Mr McClancy tell them she is a spy, and it all top-secret stuff.

Cedric just say well, well, well again. Then he say he think he remember a red sports car coming out the gate very fast one day, too. It nearly knock me down, he say, and all he remember seeing is a woman dressed in black.

Mrs McClancy say she will be having good reason to be dressed in black if she get hold of her.

She tell everybody to go to bed then, and Cedric say goodnight too, but I am still awake trying to remember all the words of 'La La La La' when I hear the fight starting. Maybe this be better than Collins v Eubank, I think, so I listen.

How did your business meeting go tonight? she ask when Mr McClancy come in. Oh fine, he say, fine, he is in the middle of very complicated negotiations. Oh yes, say his wife, complicated negotiations. Yes, he say, very detailed stuff. Oh yes, she say, very detailed stuff.

A lot of nitty-gritty, he say. Oh yes, of course, nitty gritty, say Mrs McClancy.

Then Mr McClancy say it sound like there is an echo in the room. Mrs McClancy say, oh probably, but that easy to explain. He say how do you mean? And she say maybe it because the acoustics are not as good as the Point Depot.

What? he say. You heard, she say. What kind of eejit are you? she say. It one thing, she say, sneaking off with your fancy woman, but it another thing when you parade her in front of three hundred million people for all of Dublin to see.

Mr McClancy say wait a minute now, wait a minute, you have it all wrong, dear. She say don't dear me, you know how much I tried to get tickets for that show.

He say listen, it very simple, I was at an urgent business meeting like I said, and Ms Wilde was at that meeting too. She give us valuable advice on a complicated development plan.

Huh, say Mrs McClancy, she pretty well-developed herself I notice, and why you call her Ms Wilde? Mr McClancy say things at a very sensitive stage, and Mrs McClancy say huh again. Very sensitive, she can imagine, she say.

Mr McClancy say you have it all wrong Bunny, but she say, don't Bunny me, it's you that have it all wrong this time because the camera does not lie.

Oh yes it do, he say. Are you going to tell me, she ask that that was not you in the audience with this, this, jezebel?

Mr McClancy say that it all happen at the last minute. When the meeting end, he say, Ms Wilde tell him she have been winning some tickets for the Eurovision in the Lotto (they have a small Lotto here, mama y papa, not like our great Il Gordo which of course our family never enter because we want the poor people to win instead). But, say Mr McClancy, she have been let down by some person and now she have a spare ticket.

Mrs McClancy say was it her husband who let her down, but Mr McClancy say no, one of her sisters. Oh really, she say, have she got a lot of sisters as well? Oh yes, say Mr McClancy, all lovely people.

Mrs McClancy say lovely, lovely, then why don't you invite them all around for tea some evening, dearie? He say maybe I will, dear. Then I think she throw something at him.

It sound heavier than the small coffee table this time.

Chapter 29

Ola!

Everybody in Ireland have forgotten the Eurovision already, mama y papa. Even Mrs McClancy, I think. It is because they hear Prince Charles is coming!

Mrs McClancy get so excited when she hear it that I think at first she mean he is coming to this house.

The Irish people are not having any royal families here for many years, except for St Jack Charlton of course. So everybody is talking when they hear the news that the English Prince of Wales is coming to visit them. I tell them that we in Spain are having a much more handsomer royal family with King Juan Carlos, but they are not knowing much about him here. They know about the English royal family because they read about them all the time in the papers, especially the scandals which happen every week.

Mr McClancy is wondering at the breakfast table if Camilla will be arriving too. Maybe he sneak her in on the sly, he say. Then Mrs McClancy come down the stairs and ask what that about sneaking on the sly, but he say oh nothing, nothing. Mrs McClancy say well, she is looking forward to meeting the Prince when he throw his party in the garden.

Mr McClancy say that will be the day, but he not say which day. I look in the paper later and it not say there either.

He is saying some other strange things, too, he call him the Charlie formerly known as Prince. He say he only go to the party in the garden if Di there. He say she remind him of Sally O'Brien and the way she might look at him. I think this a very strange thing to say in front of Mrs McClancy, but she just say you wouldn't look up from your harp. I tell him I never know he play a musical instrument. Mrs McClancy say then oh yes, he always pulling strings.

Theo and Cleo are asking will the little princes be coming, too. Cleo say she hope they come to visit their school, and Theo say yes, he like to shove their heads down the toilets. He thinks they are nancy boys. Mrs McClancy tell him he is not to talk like that, and he say she is right, maybe it be better not to push their heads down the toilet because their crowns block the plumbing.

Cleo say well at least Derek Derrigan not wear a crown and Theo say shh shh. Mrs McClancy stop reading about Prince Charles in the paper and ask what is that about Derek? She hope they have not been pushing his head down any more toilets. Cleo say no, it the same toilet.

This make Mr and Mrs McClancy both start shouting together at Theo. Why is he doing this again? And he say that it because this time he make jokes about Mrs McClancy and the fashion show. Mr McClancy say that no reason to push somebody's head in the toilet bowl, but Mrs McClancy just say good boy, but don't do it again. Also, she ask did he pull the chain.

Then she say to Mr McClancy, what are we going to do about Ashling's wedding? He say he want a quiet affair and she say I know that, but what about the wedding? Mr McClancy bite his toast and say it what Dick and Ash want as well, because they not want it all over the papers and the television, especially the photographs. She only have two months to go, he say.

Mrs McClancy say he have a point there. She have been able to hide the bump behind a guitar or behind bunches of flowers when people take her picture so far, but a wedding dress always get special attention. She is

111

glad they decide to go to England for a few days. They are being gone there to make more recordings.

Mr McClancy say the trouble is all the priests here are being all booked up for weddings, so maybe they get their old friend Father Seamus to do one early in the morning in Cognito. I look at the map later but not find it.

Maybe we invite him around for dinner some evening, Mrs McClancy say, and some more friends too. Mr McClancy say okay, and maybe he like to meet Haysoos in person. Then he laugh and ask if I like to show them some Spanish cooking specialities. I say yes, mama y papa, which mean *si*, so maybe you send me some recipes quickly.

We are talking about Prince Charles later in the class. Mercedes ask why are Irish people talking so much about someone else's prince when it is a republic? Conchubhair tell us that there are republicans and republicans. I ask him do that mean two republicans or many republicans, but he say it a figure of speech. I say yes, but which figure?

He say that many Irish people have a secret love for the royal family of England. I am wondering if this what Mims and Barbara mean when they send the card to the committee, because now I know they are Ms Mimble and Mrs Lemming. Maybe they have to leave the country because someone find out they love the royal family. But when I say this to Mercedes she laugh and say I have come down with the last shower.

I ask her what she mean by that, and she say it is just a figure of speech she learn from her family on the Northside. I ask her do they use shower very often and she say oh yes, they are very clean, do not listen to what Conchubhair say.

Conchubhair ask what did she say, but she say it a private discussion. He say, well please discuss your privates after the class. Then he ask us if we bring our newspapers with us to learn from the news. He say he hope we can find some pages without Mr Windsor on them. Mercedes tell me that mean Prince Charles again.

Conchubhair ask if anyone have any questions about things they see in the papers. Someone else in the class read out loud about Councillor Dithers In Nun Zoning Row. It say an order of nuns may get a million-pound windfall if one councillor change his vote at next Monday's meeting. I am wondering if Councillor Dithers is the councillor I hear Mr McClancy talking about, but I never hear this name before even in Ireland.

But what is windfall, ask the other student. Conchubhair explain that it is a figure of speech. That make three figures I have been hearing today, mama y papa. Then he say that it is like when the apples are falling off the trees and people are picking them up. But it really mean money, he say, a bit like winning the Lotto.

He say that the nuns are hoping one councillor will be voting to let some rich people get richer by building many houses on their land instead of keeping it like a park. Then they will get lots of money to help the poor people, he say. Someone ask what poor people, but Conchubhair just say when he went to the nuns as a small boy they always teach him that God is helping them that is helping themselves. Then he give one of his laughs, so maybe it is another figure of speech.

Conchubhair tell us that it is very complicated business because there are wheels within the wheels. When he say this I am thinking of the wheels of Ms Wilde's sports car, but he is saying that he have friends who like it to be a place for the travelling people to stop travelling. But that, he say, will be causing the ructions.

Then he have to explain what is ructions. When he is finished, someone else in the class ask him what is scam. She read in the papers that Gardaí Are Probing Huge BES Laundering Scam. Conchubhair ask do anyone in the class know. I say that BES is the electricity company but I not know what scam is.

But Mercedes laugh and say that is the ESB. She know what BES mean because she hear her Irish family talk about it. They argue, she say, late at night, and wake her up. Some of them want to be in a BES scheme which make them a lot of money, but other people say put it in the bank. Then the first person say oh no, not the bank, it might get robbed. Then they all laugh. But the first man is saying that the BES he talk about is as safe as houses. They laugh again then.

Nobody in the class know what scam is, so Conchubhair is telling us it is like a trick for making money vanish from your pocket. Some people are picking your pocket, but other people are being more sophisticated. Everybody in the class is writing down sophisticated, and I ask what does this big word mean? Conchubhair say it was once meaning false and artificial, but now it change its meaning. Today, he say, people want to be sophisticated so they can be looking down on other people. Oh yes, I say, that is why they go live in the tall apartments near the airport.

Conchubhair shake his head and walk over to the window and open it. I think he is going to jump out, but instead he just light one of his fat cigarettes.

Chapter 30

May

Ola!

Thank you for sending me the recipes for the Spanish specialities, mama y papa! I tell you later what happen when I cook them. But first I tell you about the visit of Prince Charles and how he is meeting Mrs McClancy.

I hear her telling it to the new committee when it meet again. It have some new members instead of Ms Mimble and Mrs Lemming who still not come back from Malaysia. I hear Cedric saying maybe they go to some Greek island next, but Mrs McClancy say not if Interpol catch them first.

Then she start telling everybody how she get to the gardening party for the Prince. Mrs Young is asking her is it because she put on her Camilla face, but Mrs McClancy say, oh now, jealousy get you nowhere. She say her friend at the Embassy put her on the short list. But Mrs Delayney-Hogge say she see the pictures in the papers and it not such a short list. Half of Dublin was at the bun fight, she say. She is a new member, mama y papa, and some times I not understand a word she say. And some times two words. She eat all the biscuits also, faster than anyone I ever see, including José Maria Herreros who was the champion eater of our school before he choke to death in Burger Heaven.

Cedric ask was Mr McClancy invited also but Mrs McClancy say he have to go to Switzerland on urgent business. Maybe he go skiing, say Mrs Young, he know all about the slippery slopes. But Mrs McClancy keep talking very excited, saying that he much taller than she expect, and very tanned.

Mrs Delayney-Hogge ask what did he say, and Mrs McClancy say oh we had quite a chat. Mrs Young ask did he mistake her flowery hat for a rosebush, which he usually talk to, but Mrs McClancy not hear her again because she say it very quietly.

Cedric ask if he playing much polo these days, but Mrs McClancy say she not bring up the subject. She just tell him, she say, that he is welcome to our little country.

The other new member, Mr Ó Farrigoch, put down his cup suddenly and say he not sit here and listen to any more of this. Everyone ask him what wrong, and he say Mrs McClancy is asking this little German upstarter to come back and take over where his great-grandparents are leaving off.

Mrs McClancy ask what he mean about a German, which I have been nearly asking myself, but Mr Ó Farrigoch say it well known that the Windsors change their name from the German Battenberg. They change their name from a cake to a soup, he say. Mrs Delayney-Hogge say what wrong with being German? She tell Mr Ó Farrigoch it was all right with his crowd during the Emergency. Then she say something about another British royalty-type person, I think. His name is Lord Ho-Ho.

Mr Ó Farrigoch say again he not going to sit here listening to this, but Cedric say wait, wait, he just the kind of person they need to help them fight the landlord class. Mr Ó Farrigoch sit down again then and drink more tea which I am pouring. It is the tea which they are growing in the south on the Barry plantation. Conchubhair tell me it is being owned by one of the merchant princes. They richer than real princes, he say.

Mrs McClancy is still talking about Prince Charles, saying he have very blue eyes which look directly into hers. Cedric say that impossible because she is bowing so

116

much, but she keep on talking and saying the Prince hold her hand for several seconds longer than was necessary. Mrs Young say he probably fighting her off. She wonder why she see no pictures in the papers of Mrs McClancy talking to the Prince, but she say it was private audience. Cedric say that a great honour for the Prince.

Mrs Delayney-Hogge is asking now can we get down to the business, and Mrs McClancy say of course, of course, but first she tell them about the food at the gardening party. Mrs Delayney-Hogge say oh yes, of course, but Mr Ó Farrigoch say she sound worse than Loodromawn Bruton. I think he mean some relation of the Irish Taoiseach, mama y papa. He say this person give a display of a Japanese custom to the Prince when he visit Dublin Castle and it make him sick to his stomach. That is Mr Ó Farrigoch's stomach. I think he call the custom cow-towing.

Then he ask did the Prince have anything to say about these latest rumours about our friend the Councillor?

Mrs McClancy stop talking, and he say, that put a stop to your gallop. What rumours? say everyone together, and he say he hear it on good authority that the Councillor have been got at. Certain parties are twisting his arm, he say. I not sure which party this can be, mama y papa.

Then they start talking about many other things. Mrs McClancy say they have to go into the lion's den and meet the Mother Superior, but Mrs Young say she hear rumours about her, too. Cedric say, don't tell me she leap over the wall, but Mrs Young laugh and say no but she may be on her way out anyway.

Mrs McClancy say she write a letter to her from the committee. This the third one, say Cedric, but maybe she want to hear about Prince Charles too. Mr Ó Farrigoch say he prefer more direct action himself, but Mrs Delayney-Hogge say she not want her windows broken from the explosions. Everybody laugh then except Mr Ó Farrigoch.

Later that day is when I am cooking the special recipe you have sent me for the guests of the McClancys. The family say it all smell very nice when I am doing it in the kitchen. They ask me what is in it, but I tell them it is a secret from my grandmother's family, which have been a favourite of Generalissimo Franco in the old days. Mr McClancy is asking me was my grandmother also a favourite, but Mrs McClancy tell him to get out of the kitchen so I can be cooking in piece.

They go upstairs then to get ready.

The doorbell ring and they nor hear it, so I welcome the first guest. It is Cedric from the committee, who tell me he like the apron which Mrs McClancy is lending me. He go into the sitting room which Mrs McClancy call the lounge, and the doorbell is ringing again. This time it is some more friends I do not know, but Mrs McClancy come running down the stairs to meet them. They are Dr Derrigan and his wife.

Mrs McClancy say come in, come in, and now I know why she have sent Theo and Cleo to the cinema and give them money also to go to the McDonalds. Mrs Derrigan is saying this is an unexpected pleasure, but Mrs McClancy say oh no the pleasure is being all hers. She hope they forget all about the trouble with Theo and Derek. Dr Derrigan say oh that is ancient history, which make Mrs McClancy look surprised.

She start to say something else but then stop again and ask them if they like a drink. They both say they like a Ballysomething and Mrs McClancy ask me to bring them in from the fridge. Mrs Derrrigan say oh, she not know au pairs cooked for parties, but I tell them it is a special treat.

They ask who else is coming and Mr McClancy look at his watch and say it is their old friend Father Seamus who they have not seen since he come back from Australia. He is bringing a friend with him whose name is Slim. Cedric say he hope it not a crocodile.

Mrs Derrigan ask when is their daughter Ashling getting married, but Mrs McClancy is not hearing her because she start telling them about how she meet Prince Charles again, and I go out to the kitchen to make sure everything is cooking nicely. We are all worrying about the time because Father Seamus not arrive yet, and I am bringing in more of the creamy Ballysomethings which the Derrigans drink with funny faces. Dr Derrigan say this must be a new version and have some more.

At last the doorbell ring and it is Father Seamus with his friend. She is very nice-looking and much taller than him, but he is not wearing the high heels. Everybody stop talking when they come in, and then they all start talking again very fast. The friend of Father Seamus is called Slim, and she hold onto his elbow so I think at first maybe she not see very well. She is also smoking many cigarettes, and Mrs McClancy keep putting the ashtray beside her, which she miss.

When they are all sitting down I am bringing in the dinner which everybody say is very nice. I am also pouring the wine, which they also say is very nice. Dr Derrigan tell everybody he appreciate a good Rioja, and Slim is saying she never smoke them herself. Seamus laugh so loud he nearly choke on my grandmother's special recipe. Slim say she hope she won't be having to do the Heimlich manoeuvre again, and Cedric say please, not in front of the guests.

When they are all drinking the coffee and the brandies, Dr Derrigan is telling Mr and Mrs McClancy what a great lad their Theo is, helping their Derek fight those bullies at school who have been taking his lunch money. Mrs McClancy look surprised again but smile and say not at all. Seamus is asking how is the new broom up at the convent, but Mrs McClancy say no, they still have the same old battle axe.

Then Mrs Derrigan see me and ask what was that lovely recipe? I tell her that it a secret again but she say she insist. But is sound more like she is saying inshisht.

Everybody then start saying they inshisht, so I am having to tell them it is the Catalonian *Cargols Picants*.

119

Mrs Derrigan say yesh but whash in it, so I tell them, it is the piquant sauce of tomatoes, herbs and almonds, and of course the *cargots* which here are called snails. I catch them in the garden eating the little blue tablets.

That is when everybody get up and run into the bathroom and some into the kitchen. Except Cedric who is a vegetarian. I wonder where everybody gone. He say they all go to call Hughie on the great white telephone. I ask him who Hughie, but he just say it an old Australian figure of speech. Their language sound even stranger than English, mama y papa.

The Derrigans go home very soon after that. Mr and Mrs McClancy not want them to leave so soon, but Dr Derrigan say he have to phone a friend who will lend him a pump. His car look okay to me, mama y papa. He bring in some red tablets and tell everybody to take some. Then he say he will be sending the bill and drive off.

Cedric stop smiling when the McClancys come back into the room. Father Seamus is helping Slim into an armchair and giving her glasses of water. I ask if anyone like anything else but they all say no, very loud. Then everyone start saying they must be going too, but Mr McClancy tell Seamus they have a favour to ask him. He say shoot, then laugh and say, after all the poison did not work. Then he laugh and say he not mean that.

Mrs Clancy then tell him all about their daughter Ashling, except the bit about the bump which she have to hide. Then she ask will he as an old friend do the wedding. Father Seamus say of course he will be delighted. Just because he is a married man himself now do not mean he can not marry other people as well. Then he look at Slim and say of course he mean that in the liturgical sense.

Mr and Mrs McClancy look very thoughtful and sit down. Cedric say he think he will have another brandy after all.

Chapter 31

June

Ola!

Today it have been Mrs McClancy's birthday but I do not think she enjoy it, mama y papa. It is because of the crash in the front garden, I think.

But first I tell you about Mr McClancy and the Big Fellow. That is the name of a pub which he have not yet been building. You remember I tell you about this big fellow, mama y papa, who live in the house where the nuns are now. Well, today I am looking for Theo and Cleo who are hiding from me in the house, and when I hear loud music I think it is coming from Mr McClancy's room and I go in. Theo and Cleo are not in the room, but I look on the table and see many nice pictures of the nun house. I think at first maybe this is a birthday present for Mrs McClancy because at breakfast she is saying she not expect anybody to remember what day it is. Mr McClancy say of course it is Tuesday, but he wink at everybody else.

But the pictures make it look not like the nun house any more, mama y papa, because it have a big sign on the roof saying THE BIG FELLOW and a big picture of a big man with a big hat.

The picture also show many houses which look very nice, with trees and ladies with buggies and many shops. Someone have been writing the word Dunes on one of the big shops, but someone else is then writing Saint

Burys over it. Mr McClancy come in then and not see me because I look for Theo and Cleo under the bed. He talk on the phone to someone and say BES a lot of times. I come out and say be very careful.

He nearly drop the phone when he see me. Then he ask me very loud what I do under the bed. I tell him I look for Theo and Cleo, but then I tell him what Conchubhair say about the BES trick that make money vanish from your pocket. Mr McClancy start to laugh then and say that will be the day. He then pick up the phone again and say sorry to it. Then he say no the job is oxo. He listen for a minute and then say again the job is really oxo, he have everything under control. His hand shake a bit then and he say, wait now there is no need to be taking that attitude.

He tell me to get out then but when I am at the door he shout wait a minute. I think he mean me but he is shouting at the phone again. He say he not need any protection thank you very much. Then he say no the gardaí have not being at the house, but then he say, yes that is long ago when the car is being stolen, but it not really stolen at all. He say yes you should know all about that sort of thing. Then he laugh and put the phone down but his hand still shake a bit.

He not see me go out. I am still hearing the loud music but it is not coming from any rooms. Where Theo and Cleo gone, I wonder, and I go looking all over the house again. Then I go up into the attic, mama y papa, and there they are, with the turntables and the records, playing the loud music. They are pretending to be a radio station, mama y papa! Theo is having a microphone and saying into it, and now here is the weather for the South Bay Area from our gorgeous weather girl Cleo. She put her hand out the window and then say it is raining.

Someone ring the front door bell then and I go down and open it. It is a boy who ask is this South Bay Radio. It is a boy from Theo's school and he have some records with him. He want to go up and play radio stations with him, so I say OK. He go up into the attic then and play his records. It very funny game, mama y papa. His name is Cornelius McGillicuddy but he call himself Brad Bryson. Theo say that silly because he already call himself Brad Brady.

Mrs McClancy is coming in then and saying she have to go to the supermarket but she suppose nobody want to help. I say I go in the car, and Theo and Cleo say they come too. She say well, well this is a surprise, that all her birthdays are coming together. She shout it again louder up the stairs, but Mr McClancy not hear because he is talking on the phone again.

We go in his big car because Mrs McClancy have a small car which she have sent to the garage man for fixing because it is sick. When he tow it away Mr McClancy say he hope I have not been feeding it any Spanish specialities.

When we finish at the shop and drive home again, Mrs McClancy suddenly remember that she have to visit the nuns, because she get a letter from the Mother Superior. We say we wait in the car, but when the nice nun at the door see us she say bring the children in too. I go in but Theo and Cleo say they listen to the radio in the car.

So I wait in room with many holy pictures and holy books for a long time. Then Mrs McClancy come back in with a nun who look not so nice. But she say she hope I am liking Ireland. I say, yes thank you. The nun shake Mrs McClancy's hand then and say she will see what she can do. She is on her side, but maybe it all out of her hands now. Mrs McClancy say thank you very much. We are going then, but at the door I am asking the nun where is old battle axe Mrs McClancy talk about.

The nun make a very strange face then and say to Mrs McClancy, we are not in the antique business. Then she shut the door.

I am telling Mrs McClancy that my grandmother's house have many antiques but she tell me to get into the car. When I do that, I get a surprise. On the radio I hear Brad Bryson saying welcome everybody to South Bay Radio, and Theo and Cleo are laughing and bouncing on the seats.

Mrs McClancy say turn off that noise and drive very fast back home. When we turn into the driveway she nearly hit the gate. That is when she see the sports car outside the door and start screaming. I have her now, she shout, and she crash Mr McClancy's car into the sports car!

I am not hurt, mama y papa, but the two cars are. Especially the sports car. Mrs McClancy jump out and shout where is she, where is she? Mr McClancy shout who, who? Mrs McClancy shout, the woman who own that car, where is she?

Mr McClancy say, I'm looking at her.

Then he hand her the keys and say, happy birthday dear.

Chapter 32

Ola!

I have being to another Irish wedding, but this one was not being the same as the other one. At first there was only one man with a video camera, but then suddenly, mama y papa, there were many!

Also this time I am being the best man.

The wedding of Ashling and Dick is not having many guests, maybe because it is early in the morning. I ask Mrs McClancy if her sister Birdie not come to it, but Mr McClancy say she have to get out of her cage first.

I think it funny when they call me the best man when it is Dick who is getting married, but that is what they are calling it here when you help with the rings. When I am giving Dick the rings he say give me five man, but I tell him I am only having two.

Ashling look very nice and carry a very big bunch of flowers. The priest is Father Seamus who look very tired, I think. He ask if anybody in the church know why this couple should not be married. Nobody say anything, because only the McClancys and the video man and some people from Dick's band are in the church. Then Theo jump up in his seat but Mrs McClancy put her hand over his mouth and pull him down again.

When the wedding is over Mrs McClancy cry a little bit, but say to Mr McClancy, well at least the media did not find out about it. But when we go out the door of the church, mama y papa, the cameras they are everywhere. Also many reporters who are running around in little circles and talking into the little telephones and the big microphones.

Dick and Ashling are running to get into their car, and Ashling is nearly tripping over her dress and letting fall the very big flowers. Mrs McClancy is saying oh oh, and damn damn, but then I see all the reporters and the camera people turning around and running the other way.

They are not taking pictures of Dick and Ashling at all, but of Father Seamus who is getting into a nice shiny car. There is already a driver in the car. I am glad to see it is Slim, who is well again.

All the camerapersons are taking many pictures of Slim who wave and smile at them and lean out the window to say hello boys. The reporters are asking her many questions. I think she work in the fishing business before she come here because someone shout and ask is she a hooker, but she say no she is being a nightclub hostess, but Father Seamus save her. He keep telling Slim to drive, drive, but she keep smiling for the cameras. He open the window and shout he see them all in court. That is all I see then because Mrs McClancy grab me and pull me into the taxi they use because their cars still are being broken up.

The taximan have lots of money on the seat. Mr McClancy ask him where it come from and he say oh he get it from tips. Mr McClancy say it look more like tip-offs.

The next morning at the breakfast table, Mr and Mrs McClancy are looking at the papers and saying well it could have being worse. The wedding of Dick and Ashling get mentioned, but all the papers are having only big colour pictures of Father Seamus and Slim, except they are calling her another name by mistake, which is Bimbo From Oz.

Then Mrs McClancy give a little scream and I think she burn her mouth on the egg I am boiling for her. But it is not the egg. She have seen something else in the paper. It is not about about the wedding, it is about the Council which meet last night. The place they meet sounds very Spanish, mama y papa – the paper say COUNCILLORS IN FURORE AS REZONING IS REVERSED.

Mr McClancy not look upset at all. He is reading another paper which say PRESIDENT TO VISIT NUNS IN CONTROVERSY CONVENT.

I am the only person who is reading the front page which say FOX MAY BE ELECTED. When we talk about this in the class later, I am saying it is a very strange country to have a fox in the elections, but he say that nothing, Ireland already have a rabbit in the Government. And, he say, they throw poor Alberto to the wolves but the chickens now are coming home to roost. When I say it is very strange to have so many animals, he say they also have many vegetables. So you see, mama y papa, that Irlanda is still being an agricultural country.

Conchubhair is asking me where is the book of Irish history which he is lending me earlier, but I think I leave it somewhere because I am not finding it in the McClancy house when I look high and low. I even look in the attic where Theo and Cleo not have their radio station any more.

I forget to tell you in all the excitements that Mr and Mrs McClancy go mad when they find out it is not a toy radio station but a real one. They find out when more boys and girls are coming to the door with their records and saying they are deejays. Then they ask where is the radio.

Mr McClancy jump up and down in the kitchen when he ask Theo and Cleo about it. He ask Theo and Cleo where they getting the money to pay these boys, but Theo explain that it work the other way – the boys and girls are paying Theo and Cleo to let them be deejaying for an hour. Mr McClancy say, holy God you'll have us all arrested, and he tell them to get that stuff out of the house.

Theo say he sell it because he tired of being a radio station anyway. Cleo say maybe Derek Derrigan buy the stuff off them, and Theo say yes, if he ask him nicely, but Mr McClancy not hear them because he answer the phone and talk about an urgent meeting.

When I am coming back from the class I remember that maybe I have Conchubhair's book the day I go to the convent with Mrs McClancy. I think maybe I leave it there on the table when we are going home quickly and not seeing the battle axe.

So I am going to visit the convent again, and maybe this time also I will be seeing the famous battle axe. I am coming to the convent from the back gate and that is when I am seeing something I will warn the nuns about – they have been leaving a ladder up on the back wall of the convent, and another one on the roof. With so many buglers we read about every day in the papers, I am afraid maybe the nuns will be bugled by leaving these ladders.

I think I hear buglers in the bushes when I get near to the convent, because it sound like someone laughing and running away. It even sound a bit like Theo, but then I think no, maybe it one of those foxes or rabbits.

I am seeing something else strange, too, mama y papa. There is a big shed made of wood at the back of the convent also, and I am thinking that this where the ladders are coming from. But when I look in the door, I see there is a sports car there instead, and now I am thinking that maybe the nuns have a garage business and they are fixing Mrs McClancy's birthday present.

But Mr McClancy is doing it as another surprise for her, because when I am coming around the side of the house, who is coming out the door but Mr McClancy. He is smiling and waving and going down the steps and saying but everything now look stitched up, and he hope there be no leaks. Then he walk away down the driveway, because his own car being fixed in some other garage.

128

I knock on the door then and when a nun come I tell her about Conchubhair's book. She go and find it for me. Then I ask if I can see the old battle axe, but she start to laugh so much I think she never stop. Then she tell me the old battle axe is gone. They have a new broom, like Father Seamus say they have.

I tell her then about the ladders, but she say oh that is only Batman!

Chapter 33

Ola!

Help, mama y papa! I am writing this letter to you but not knowing when you will get it. I explain from the start, but I am not even sure what I am explaining about the terrible things that have being happening here.

It all start, I think, when Mrs McClancy is hearing that the President is coming to visit the nuns in the convent I tell you about already. She is having another meeting of the committee to talk about how they give her a warm welcome, and I am writing down some of the big words they use.

Mrs Delayney-Hogge say, oh yes, I think we make it really hot for her that day. I am wondering how they make it hot here in Ireland, mama y papa, because I have been wearing many of my underpants and vests every day since I am arriving. But then Cedric say he hopes they not be too hard on Mary as it not her fault the nuns are selling out to the fat cats.

Mr Ó Farrigoch say that for once he agree with Cedric, but he say that the visit is a big chance to hog the cameras. Then he say sorry to Mrs Delayney-Hogge. Mrs McClancy say oh of course she have nothing against the President personally, she is getting a Christmas card from her every year, but it will be a chance to picket and protest in the full glare of the world's media.

Mrs Young say steady on there, we be lucky if there is being one reporter from the *Irish Catholic* and someone with a microphone in an anorak from East Coast Radio.

By the way, she say, have anyone heard that pirate radio that interrupt Classic FM all the time. Mr Ó Farrigoch say it a pity about her and her Classic FM, but what about the housing protest?

Cedric say he think they picket the Councillor's house as well, and he wonder how the BES boys got at him to switch. Mrs Delayney-Hogge say it all a shocking business. Now I think maybe they are talking about electricity again after all.

Mrs Young say no, we should keep away from the Councillor's home because we not want people to mix us up with the pro-life extremists. Mr Ó Farrigoch put down his cup and ask what wrong with that, but Mrs McClancy clap her hands and say now now, boys and girls, that is not why we are being here. Mr Ó Farrigoch say we boys and girls are lucky to be here at all the way some people think. Cedric say ouch, even though I am not spilling the tea on him.

Mrs McClancy say look here we must be getting the public on our side so we still get this decision reversed. She say she is planning our demonstration in meticulous detail. Mrs Young say oh yes, like the fashion show.

Cedric then ask, by the way have anyone heard from Mims and Barbara because their money running out soon. Mrs McClancy say it not their money, it our money and she hope they are becoming destitute in some godforsaken hellhole. Mrs Young say that sound like the houses the fat cats are wishing to build next door. Mrs Delayney-Hogge say yes she can not be imagining how people can live in such little concrete boxes packed in together. We must stamp out this exploitation, she say.

Mrs McClancy say that is the very thing she was going to say. We get up a petition she say, and hand it to the President when she comes out of the convent. Maybe that embarrass the nuns so they not sell. Mr Ó Farrigoch say yes but that not enough. We rally the troops, he say. Cedric say he not know there are being soldiers there, but

Mr Ó Farrigoch say he speaking metaphorically. Then he suddenly ask me am I spying on him. I say no but I write words down for Conchubhair.

Who is this Conchubhair, he shout and jump up. But Mrs McClancy explain that he is my teacher. Mr Ó Farrigoch sit down again then, but say you can't be too careful nowadays. Cedric then pick up the flowers and say, testing, testing over and out. Everyone laugh except Mr Ó Farrigoch

I go out then to answer the phone, and Cedric shout mind the bugs. It is Mercedes on the phone. She have not being at school for few days, and I wonder where she is. But she say oh just a cold, but now she is okay and want to talk about the President coming to visit. Mercedes want me to bring her to the convent that day, because she collect the names of famous people. I tell her I am not being that famous, but she laugh and say she know I will help her get the President to sign her book. I say yes of course but there be many policemen in case there be trouble.

Mercedes say she will not be making any trouble. I tell her no, it is Mrs McClancy who will be making it.

Then Mercedes suddenly ask what is that funny noise on your phone. I ask what funny noise, and then I hear the music. It is a Boyzone record and it sound very far away. But it is coming from the phone, and then I hear someone say South Bay Area FM. It sound like Theo.

I shout hello, hello very loud, but Mercedes say she not deaf. I am explaining that I think I hear a radio on the phone and am trying to talk to it, but she start laughing and say that is why she is liking me, I always make her smile, not like Conchubhair. Then she say bye-bye she have to go and do some washing. I hope it not her hair again and she say no, just some clothes.

I am asking why is she washing the clothes when her Irish family are having a laundry, but she say she think they are closing it down soon. She not understand everything they say when she hear them talking about it, because then one of them also say he not want to go on any long holidays but he also say the heat getting too much here.

I am not understanding this either, but I hope they not come over here because Mrs McClancy and her friends are making it a very hot day when the President is coming.

Chapter 34

Ola!

Help again, mama y papa! I send this letter with the last one which I stop writing when it get dark. Maybe you get them all together.

The day the President is coming, nobody can find Theo and Cleo anywhere, mama y papa! I look in their beds but they are not there, and I think maybe they were not sleeping there the night before because they have been putting pillows sleeping there instead.

Mr McClancy is wondering where they go, but he tell me to phone their friends and find out if they are there. He is too busy today of all days, he say. Mrs McClancy say she is also too busy getting her picket ready. She ask Mr McClancy if he come with the residents, but he laugh and say, oh that bunch, no thanks. He have very important persons to meet, he say. Big deal, say his wife. Yes, a very big deal, say Mr McClancy. He hope to clinch it this morning.

Mrs McClancy say it make a change that he be thinking of that kind of clinch. He say she have a one-track mind, then he go on reading the paper. It say REZONING PROTESTS TO MAR MARY'S CONVENT CUPPA.

I am going and phoning some friends of Theo and Cleo, but nobody see them. But Derek Derrigan say he hear Theo on the radio that morning talking about Boyzone. I ask him what radio, and he say oh maybe I should not be telling you that, now I be getting the bowl again. Then he hang up.

I am telling Mr and Mrs McClancy I go out to look for Theo and Cleo, but first I go upstairs and put on my best sweater for meeting Mercedes at the gate of the convent. There are many policemen there already, and a big crowd is outside the gates. Some of them are on their holidays, I think, because they have stopped and parked their caravans to wait and see the President when she arrive.

I am getting a big surprise when I see Mr McClancy standing inside the gate. I am getting another surprise when I see him talking to one of the policemen, because he look like the policeman who ask me all the questions the time I go over to the Northside and get lost. Mr McClancy see me coming in the gate. Then then he point at me and say in a loud voice to the policeman, there is your major criminal now. Then he wink at me and laugh. But the policeman not laugh.

I am looking for Mercedes and walking around the convent when I see the ladders are still being up at the back. This surprise me, but then I remember the nun who joke about Batman. I take the ladders down in case the buglers come, but maybe not today when there so many policemen. I look up at the sky because I know the President is coming in a helicopter today. Mr McClancy say it really a flying visit.

That is why I am nearly being knocked down by her car when she arrive. It is coming very quickly in the gate and there is much shouting and screaming. I think at first they are all shouting and sceaming because I am nearly being knocked down. I fall into some long green weeds and get lost for a while. They are called nettles, mama y papa, and they are worse than the scorpions.

Suddenly I am being very itchy and bumpy on my face and my hands, but I crawl out to see the President. But I am not seeing her. She have gone into the nuns house already, but there is still much screaming and shouting at the gate. I run to see if Mercedes is there and see much fighting in the road.

There are many policemen trying to stop a big crowd of people who are waving the big placards and trying to come in the gate. The placards say SOS and Save Our Space. Some of them also say Recreation Before Speculation and No Sell-out, Sisters! Mr Ó Farrigoch have one that say Remember Davitt, No Absentee Landlords. I am thinking I ask Conchubhair about that. I see Cedric waving one that say Let Our Children Live, and I am wondering where Theo and Cleo vanish.

But they are not the only people who are at the gate. There are also many little girls who look like Cleo, and they are all screaming and crying and biting the policemen. The policemen are trying to push them back out of the gate, but some of them are getting under their legs and running up the driveway shouting Steve and Ronan.

I am stepping out to tell them that it is not Boyzone but President Robinson who own the car, but they push me back into the weeds, mama y papa! When I get out again they are climbing on the roof of the car and shouting Ronan and Keith. Also they are writing these names on the windows of the car with the lipstick. The man who drive the car is telling them to go away but they are screaming at him to give them some of his hair because he is Boyzone's friend.

He walk away very quickly when he see one of them taking out a scissors. Many policemen and cameramen are coming running up to the car then. Someone is shouting get the fire brigade, and someone else say no, get the army. The policemen are chasing the girls away from the car and they are running all over the place. A policman nearly knock me back into the weeds again, but I only get my hands stinging this time.

Then I look down to the gate and see Mrs McClancy and her friends coming in. The policemen have been too busy to stop them and they are shouting and marching up the drive. I think Mrs McClancy look like Don Quixote. Or maybe, mama y papa, she just look like his horse. She is shouting at a policeman that she have a perfect right to be here, that she have been invited by the President.

The policeman is saying sorry ma'am but he have his orders. Mr Ó Farrigoch then start shouting about the fascists, and then he is asking him what colour is his shirt. I am very puzzled by this because every policeman here is wearing a blue shirt with his uniform. The policeman take out his notebook and ask him his name, but Mr Ó Farrigoch wave a big long paper at him and shout that his name is there with the many thousands of other names.

The policeman say it look like a few dozen to him, now will he please be a good man and wait at the gate. Mr Ó Farrigoch shout who is he calling a good man? Many policemen are coming then and trying to push them back to the gates. They are also trying to push back the television cameras and the other camera people and the radio people who are also here now. I even think I am seeing the one they call Charlie.

Then I hear someone shouting my name. At first I am not sure, because so many people here are calling Jaysoos. But it is the voice of Mercedes. She is in the crowd at the gate. I run down to get her in, but the police have been putting ropes in the way. When she see my face she start screaming Jaysoos even louder, then she ask what happen to my face.

I am telling her it only the green weeds, but then Mrs McClancy see me too, and she start screaming what did the police do to you. I am telling her it is not the police, but she shout to the camerapersons, look what they do to this poor boy. I am telling her this is a great insult to the blood of my family to say I am poor, but everyone start to take pictures of me then and asking me many questions. I grab Mercedes' hand and run into the bushes to get away from them.

The little girls who think the President is Boyzone are also still in the bushes and running around screaming. But as well as the screaming of the girls and the noise from the gate, I think I hear loud music. It sound like it come from the nuns' house. They all run around to the back of the house and I start to run too, but first Mercedes catch my hand again and kiss my face, to make it better, she say. It feel a bit better then, but the policemen are coming to look for us and we run.

The music have stopped again when we get to the back of the nun's house. A man is standing there and the little girls are screaming at him because they think he know where Boyzone are hiding, but he laugh and say no he is only Batman himself. One girl shout that he look more like Robin, but he laugh again and say no he really is Batman. Someone say well, where's your ropes, and he say he just use ladders but someone steal them. The place is full of buglers, he say.

More policemen come running then and the girls scream and run into the trees. We go the other way because Mercedes is saying she want to go and get the President's name for her book. I tell her I think she not have much chance but we run to the front of the house. We are too late, the President's car is just driving away. I see some nuns looking out the window and I get a surprise, mama y papa, because one of the nuns look like Ms Wilde. Maybe she have a twin, too.

Then there is more shouting and fighting at the gate, and I see Mrs McClancy running up the drive shouting Mary, Mary it's me, we have joint friends from your days at the bar. Then a policewoman is bringing her down with a rugby tackle which is the other game they play in Lansdowne Road. The car swerve a bit then drive off very quickly.

I am thinking that maybe the cameras and the reporters and the police go away then, but there is still much fighting between Mrs McClancy's friends and the police. Cedric is hitting a very big policeman with his placard and shouting, take that big boy. The policeman is picking him up with one hand and letting him fall into the goldfish pond.

Mercedes is running to help him out and I am going too. That is when we hear more noise from the gate and see many of the holiday people with the caravans driving in. They must wish to see more of the excitement which they are missing out on the road. The camerapersons are taking lots of pictures of them, and the drivers wave and smile at them.

Now I think there will be a big fight when the policemen try to put them out again, but that is not happening. They are all driving right up to the front of the house and stopping. They all look at Cedric who is telling a policeman that he is not stealing the goldfish, he just find it in his trousers. The policeman say he is disgusting.

Then the convent doors open and out come Mr McClancy. He look very surprised when he see all the caravans. I am very surprised too, mama y papa, because the nun beside him is Ms Wilde. I know, because she look at me and wink.

Chapter 35

Ola!

I am still having a pain in my head, mama y papa, and I am not sleeping very well in this bed, that is why I stop writing last night about the terrible things that happen to me here. I hope you get these letters soon.

I get the pain in the head, I think from the sirens, or maybe from the fight that start soon after Ms Wilde say she is the new Mother Superior.

The camerapersons all take many pictures of her then, but I am still wondering what is Mr McClancy doing there on the steps and why is he having some papers and a big shiny pen. He also have a microphone. Mrs McClancy is also wondering, I think, because she have stopped practising the rugby tackles with the police woman.

Everybody go very quiet then, except the little girls who I can hear very far away crashing around in the trees and looking for Boyzone. Mercedes catch my hand and we listen to Mr McClancy talking with the microphone.

He is saying this is a historic day for everybody because they say goodbye to the nuns, but he have some good news before they go. Then he take out a cheque which he hold up to the cameras. I am not able to see it because all the camerapeople are pushing everybody else out of the way. They knock Mercedes down and are nearly walking on her, but I pull her up again and she hold on to me. I am also holding on to her so that she not fall again.

Mr McClancy is waving the cheque around and everybody is saying ooh, aah, it is for many millions of pesetas, mama y papa. He is also saying something about the how the good nuns not listen to those selfish people who want to waste all this land when so many people need somewhere to live. Ms Wilde, I mean the new Mother Superior, is nodding and smiling, but Mrs McClancy is not.

Then he give the cheque to Ms Wilde, I mean the new Mother Superior, and all the camerapersons flash their cameras and knock everybody down again. Then she take the microphone and say thank you very much to Mr McClancy for this very kind donation. Everybody clap again and Mr McClancy get his pen ready and write his name on the other piece of paper. He give them to her then and wait for her to write her name on it also.

But mama y papa, that is when the real trouble start.

Ms Wilde the Mother Superior take up the microphone again and say there have been a change of plan. She thank Mr McClancy again for the kind donation which she know he can be writing off for the taxman, but then she say this have enabled her sisters to stay after all, and she know Mr McClancy will be pleased. He not look pleased at all. I am thinking he is going to fall down off the steps. He is trying to take the microphone again, and the camerapersons are now walking on each other to take more pictures.

The Mother Superior is laughing and saying no, don't thank me till I finish. Mr McClancy is saying but but but. Then he say you don't understand, what about all those meetings we had?

Then Mercedes say look over there, here come my family from the Northside, what they doing here? But when I look, I am only seeing many politicians who are peeping out from the trees. There is El Bruton and El Bert and Alberto and El Dic, but I am not seeing any of the Thorny Generals although I am looking very closely.

I am saying to Mercedes that they are only the politicians, but she laugh and say I am blind as well as silly, they are all wearing masks, mama y papa! She say it is a game they play many times in the house where she stay. That is what she like about them, she never know who is going to open the door when she go home, sometimes it is even John Major or Bill Clinton. But she say she wish it was Brad Pitt or Johnny Depp.

I am looking sad when I hear her say this, but she squeeze my hand and say I not need any mask. Then she laugh and say of course I need one today because of the nettles making my face go bumpy.

The family of Mercedes are moving closer to the steps and looking up at Mr McClancy. The police are also moving closer and looking at them. One policeman is saying oh hello Taoiseach, we weren't expecting you, but a sergeant is saying, get back here you stupid yellowpack, can't you see he has a rubber face? The first policeman is saying that is a terrible thing to say about the Taoiseach.

Mr McClancy is getting the microphone at last and his hands shake a lot. He look around at Mercedes family and they shake even more. Then he say to the Mother Superior again that she not understand. I am thinking he is going to cry, mama y papa, when he tell her that the money is not being his to give. It represent, he say, the savings of many small investors. He look around again at Mercedes' family when he say this. They are moving very close to the steps and putting their hands in their pockets.

Ms Wilde the Mother Superior is taking the microphone again and saying she know that the many small investors will be glad when they hear what their money is being used for. Then she start telling everybody, mama y papa, that the nuns are being starting a caravan and camping park instead of the houses! I think she mean like the holiday places we see sometimes when we pass by the Costa Brava, with the many bright tents and little children splashing in the pools.

But they will be having to put in a new pool here, I think, because the one they have only really have room for some goldfish. And Cedric, who is also small.

The people who are already here in their caravans are clapping when she say this, and she is saying she is glad they could be coming. But nobody else is clapping, especially Mrs McClancy who is trying to get up onto the steps.

Also not clapping is the man I think is the Councillor. He is standing near Mercedes so I hear him talking to himsself, saying but what about the video, what about the video? Mercedes ask him what is he talking about and he look at her like someone who have been run over by a caravan. Then he say I never wanted prosperity, all I asked for was a bit of posterity. Mercedes explain to him that she not know what those big words mean. Then he say they promised to name the estate after me. He also say they were even going to put up a statue of me.

There is much shouting from the steps which are getting very crowded. Also getting up on them now are the camerapersons, reporters, some people from Mercedes' family with the masks, and also many policemen.

Mr McClancy is trying to run into the nuns' house and the men in the masks are following him. He is trying to slam the door and one of them put his foot in the way and start to push it. I am still thinking it is the one they call El Kemmy, but Mercedes say oh, oh, I think that is Cousin Anto, he the heaviest of them all.

But then Cousin Anto disappear when four policemen and a policewoman are jumping on him. But then the man in the El Bruton mask is taking the microphone and shouting stop, stop. Everybody stop except Mrs McClancy who is hitting everybody.

The man with the microphone start talking, but then a sergeant is grabbing him and trying to take off his El Bruton mask. We have you this time, he shout, and now we know how you launder the money. I am very puzzled when I hear this, because everybody know, mama y papa, that if you put the money in a washing machine, it is getting soggy. How many times have you been telling me, mama, not to be leaving the pesetas in my Levis?

The El Bruton man tell the policeman he not know what he talking about. This have all been a big mistake, he say. The sergeant say, you can say that again, but the man not hear him. No, no, he say, you must not believe this Mr McClancy, we have never been meeting him in our lives, and we not know what he mean when he say we are small investors.

The one they call Cousin Anto is shouting right, we're big investors, but someone is kicking him on the shins or somewhere and he not say anything else for a while. The microphone man is saying, no, no, youse gorrit all wrong, we are travelling entertainers and we come here today to tell the good nuns we wish to do a charity fundraising show for them. Then he start to sing 'You the Key to My Life'.

But the sergeant say rubbish – lads, get them, and he try to grab the mask again. That is when Mrs McClancy hit him by mistake and when the sergeant is wondering who hit him, Mercedes' family run away into the woods. They are having to run very fast when they get there, because the little girls have been hearing the singing and come running after them shouting Steve and Ronan why are you wearing those masks?

The policemen are all running after them, and that is when Mr McClancy is coming out the window at the side of the nuns' house. He try to tiptoe away but he not see Mrs McClancy coming until she shout, you conniving bastard and hit him with the pole of the placard.

He fall down and she hit him again, but he is shouting, who are you calling a conniving bastard you stupid cow, who do you think keeps you living beyond your means? I not know what this English means, but it really annoy

Mrs McClancy. She throw herself on top of Mr McClancy and they are rolling around in the dust with their clothes getting very untidy.

I am afraid they are killing each other, but just then some men from the caravans are coming and picking Mrs McClancy up first, and then Mr McClancy. They are still trying to fight, but the men from the caravans are strong and not letting them.

They say nothing for a while. Then one of them put out his hand to Mrs McClancy and say how do you do, we are your new neighbours. I think for a minute he say his name is Conchubhair, but it just sound a bit like it.

A horn is blowing then and I am nearly being knocked down by a car. It is the President's car again, coming back up the driveway! Mercedes catch me before I fall into the nettles again. The car pass by and it is very wet and clean and shining, like it have been going through the car wash.

I think Mrs McClancy is really going to start crying now, because the door of the convent open and out come the President. She have been in there all the time waiting for the car to come back and all the noisy people to go away. She say goodbye to the nuns and shake hands with the man from the caravan, who she know well I think.

Then she nod at Mrs McClancy. Hello Birdie, she say.

Mrs McClancy say it's Bunny but the President have got into the car and gone already.

Mrs McClancy is opening and closing her mouth like one of the goldfish.

That is when we see the big black cloud coming from the roof of the nuns' house.

Chapter 36

Ola, mama y papa

Well, that was how far I get with my last letter before my arm get tired from being in the sling.

What is happening next to our boy, you are probably asking each other, and that is what I am also asking Mercedes when we see the black cloud. Someone is shouting get the fire brigade and we all run around to the back of the nuns' house.

When I am running through the woods and holding Mercedes' hand in case she fall, I am nearly falling myself when my foot is stepping on something soft. I am looking down and seeing a face smiling up at me. I get a bad fright, mama y papa, but it is only the rubber face of El Bruton! I pick it up so that nobody else fall over it.

Maybe that is when the trouble really start.

We are arriving at the back of the house and seeing everybody looking up at the roof. And when I look up, I see someone with a very black face looking down. It is Theo.

Also with him is Cleo who not have such a black face.

They are shouting at the policemen who are shouting up at them, but it is hard to hear what they are saying because of the little girls who are all screaming the names of the Boyzone and running around in the very small circles. The camerapersons are taking pictures of everything, especially each other.

The ladders which I have been hiding from the buglers have being put back against the wall of the convent, but nobody is going up or down.

The big black cloud is coming from the window in the roof, but it is not smoke. It is bats, mama y papa. There are many thousands of them flying around and around. Mercedes is afraid they get in her hair. That probably mean she will have to start washing it again.

The police are shouting through a big horn thing at Theo and Cleo. The sergeant have it and he is saying just like *NYPD Blue* in a very loud voice Come Down With Your Hands Up We Have The Place Surrounded.

But Theo shout back, You Will Never Take Brad Brady Alive. Then he throw a slate. Cleo is also shouting South Bay FM Forever. She also throw a slate and say that's today's crash call.

The sergeant is stepping back out of the way and then saying again in his loud voice We Know You've Got The Whole Gang Up There In The Attic So Come Down Quietly.

Then a man start coming down the ladder and when he get to the ground thirty policemen and women are jumping on him. But he shout what the hell is going on, I am the Batman.

The sergeant is saying And I Am The Joker into the big horn, which give everybody a surprise, especially the sergeant. Then he say it again to the Batman with only his mouth. But the Batman is saying no you don't understand, the nuns have the bats in the attic.

The sergeant say You Could Have Fooled Me, They Seem To Be A Right Bunch Of Cute then he put the horn down again and I not hear the last word.

The sergeant is then saying where's your cloak then caped crusader, but the Batman say no really his name is Professor Peter Plumleigh from England and he have been studying the bats. That is why I not understand him so well at first, because he is speaking the English English which nobody understand. Everything was going perfectly well until those two little animals arrive last week, he say. I am wondering what little animals he mean, but just then two more slates are breaking on the ground beside us.

Those little beasts, say the Professor, have ruined my work with their awful ghetto-blaster so-called music.

The sergeant turn around to shout back with his horn again, and a man with a microphone is asking the Professor but why did you let the little gurriers into the attic in the first place? The Professor say I did not let them in, they told me the nuns let them in because they come from a deprived background and need some place to play their music. Then, he say, they have being pretending they have a radio station and he have been quite amused really at first. Even the bats, he say, have enjoyed the music.

But what happen this morning, the microphone man is asking. The Professor is shrugging his shoulders and say he not know for sure, but he think that is the first time they play a record by some ghastly person called Dick O'Lashnikoff.

It is driving my nuts bats, he say. Or maybe he say it the other way around. It is a figure of speech, mama y papa. Then two things are happening. I hear the sound of a fire engine coming very close. The siren is sceaming because it is coming up the driveway. But the noise is not so loud as the noise from the little girls who think they have found Boyzone in the nuns garage.

There is even more noisier screaming then from someone else. It is the men they have found who are not Boyzone. That sound like one of my family, say Mercedes, he make that noise before when he play the party game called Where's The Bleedin Loot with Cousin Anto.

The police and the camerapersons and the microphone people are all running to the noise, but I wait to see the fire engine coming to the front of the nuns' house and I go with Mercedes to tell them it is not on fire after all. But we do not get there because we meet Mrs McClancy who come running around and shouting at me what have you done with my poor children. Then she start to shake me by the shoulders.

Mr McClancy come running around too, and he try to make her stop but she punch him in the face and go on shaking me. She is shouting that it all my fault. Mercedes is shouting that everything is okay, but she not listen until the fire brigade people nearly knock her down with the hosepipe.

They run around the back and point the hose up at the roof. I think they will be drowning Theo and Cleo with the water, but just then I see them coming down the Batman ladder and running around the other side of the house.

Mrs McClancy is not seeing them, and I am afraid she will catch me again to shake me, so I run after them, but first I feel something in my pocket. It is the El Bruton mask which I am putting on so that she think I am the Taoiseach. She will not be shaking him by the shoulders, I think.

That is when I am nearly being knocked into some more of the nettles, mama y papa, by another car. It is not the President's car coming back again, but the sports car of Ms Wilde the Mother Superior. It have the roof down. And it is being driven by the Government, mama y papa.

Well, that is what it look like at first, because it is so crowded. Only one of them is driving of course, but all the other men are sitting on the seats or on the back of the car, except the big one who is lying on the boot and holding on to the back of the seats with his fingers. He is nearly falling off because he is also kicking at the little girls who are running after him and catching his trousers.

He is screaming louder than them and he is saying Are Youze All As Blind As Bats Or What? Do I Look Like Steve Out Of Boyzone? Can't Youze See I'm Jim Effinkemmy?

It is Cousin Anto and his friends. They are all wearing their masks again.

The police are trying to catch them, but the little girls are all getting in their way. Then one of the police shout, hey, there's one of them there. He is talking about me, mama y papa!

I try to tell him that I am Jésus, but of course he not believe me because he think I am El Bruton. Many policemen are coming after me then, so I am running around the side of the house. I jump onto the side of the fire engine which is just driving away. I am pulling open the door to climb in when someone try to hit me with a hatchet. It is Cleo. And the driver is Theo.

Chapter 37

Ola!

It is autumn here now, and I think this is my last letter for a while, mama y papa.

After the fire engine crash when the bats all land on the windows I have been learning many new words.

I do not mean the words of the driver of the bus, mama y papa, because I do not think many of them were English. But I have learned many other big words since they brought me here after going to the hospital.

I am looking forward to using these words many times when I get back home to Madrid, but I am not sure when that will be. Here are some of the words:

Obstructing a Member of the Force in the Pursuance of His or Her Duties.

Abducting a Minor.

Abducting Another Minor.

Allowing Oneself To Be Carried in an Illegally Driven Vehicle.

Assisting in the Taking Without Permission of Said Vehicle, To Wit, a Fire Engine, the Property of the Municipal Authorities.

Causing Damage to an Omnibus.

Affray.

Assault.

Battery.

Inciting a Riot.

Causing the Destruction of a Colony of Bats, a Species Protected by Irish and European Law.

Defacing the President's Car.

Assisting in the Escape of Persons Suspected of Criminal Activities.

Cruelty to a Goldfish.

Impersonating the Taoiseach of the Day.

They are just some of the words I learn from the judge, who is a very nice man. When I start talking he send for an interpreter. I tell him it okay, my English is very good now because I learn it from the McClancys. He explain that the interpreter is not for me, it is for him.

Other words I learn are Remand and Bail. I am hoping Mr McClancy is coming with some money for the judge. Maybe I make a mistake when I use the word Bribe instead of Bail, but the judge say he understand the difference.

The sergeant is explaining to him that the McClancy family have gone on holidays. This surprise me because they never are saying it to me.

Mercedes say her family, too, have been going on their holidays very suddenly, but she have found a new place to stay. I ask her if it is with Conchubhair, but she laugh and laugh, and say no it is being worse than that. It is the convent.

When she is telling the nuns about where I am now, Ms Wilde the Mother Superior is saying she put the wheels in motion for me. But I hope she is not coming in the sports car, mama y papa.

Anyway, the food is much better here than I get in the McClancy house.

And Mercedes say she will wait for me.

Your loving son,
Jesús de Arriba y Labamba